TALKS on NATIONALISM

EDWARD BELLAMY

"The American people are right in demanding New Nationalism, without which we cannot hope to deal with new problems. The New Nationalism puts the national need before sectional or personal advantage. It is impatient of the utter confusion that results from local legislatures attempting to treat national issues as local issues. It is still more impatient of the impotence which springs from overdivision of governmental powers, the impotence which makes it possible for local selfishness or for legal cunning, hired by wealthy special interests, to bring national activities to a deadlock. This New Nationalism regards the executive power as the steward of the public welfare. It demands of the judiciary that it shall be interested primarily in human welfare rather than in property, just as it demands that the representative body shall represent all the people rather than any one class or section of the people."—Theodore Roosevelt in The New Nationalism (1910).

Edward Bellamy

TALKS

on

NATIONALISM

BY

EDWARD BELLAMY

". . . ye can discern the face of the sky;
but can ye not discern the signs of the
times?"—Matthew 16:3.

Select Bibliographies Reprint Series

BOOKS FOR LIBRARIES PRESS
FREEPORT, NEW YORK

First Published 1938
Reprinted 1969

STANDARD BOOK NUMBER:
8369-5111-5

LIBRARY OF CONGRESS CATALOG CARD NUMBER:
78-102226

PRINTED IN THE UNITED STATES OF AMERICA

TABLE OF CONTENTS

TABLE OF CONTENTS—*Continued*

Foreword

by

WILLIAM P. HARVEY

"The movement toward the conduct of business by larger and larger aggregations of capital, the tendency toward monopolies, which had been so desperately and vainly resisted, was recognized at last, in its true significance, as a process which only needed to complete its logical evolution to open a golden future to humanity." (Edward Bellamy in "Looking Backward.")

I

THERE is in the United States today an intellectual stir over social and economic matters such as was evident in the 1880s. At that time, the country entered a new social and economic era in the first impact between a leisured and competent citizenry, who were largely their own keepers, and the *new industrialism.*

Without detail, it may be said this nation had by that time reached a full period as a people with endless frontiers, as men and women free to order their lives as they willed and to find sustenance from the generous breasts of Nature. The smoke of many factory chimneys soiled an air that had been open to sun and cloud.

The days of man's dependence on his fellows had arrived. The great and seemingly infinite resources of the land had been garnered safely into the keeping of the comparatively few. Those lusty young men and women who soon after adolescence might with axe and hoe carve out a full, even if simple, existence in the preceding generation and so raise families of new pioneers, found "No Trespass" signs over the great regions their fathers had passed over with hastening feet.

9

FOREWORD

Our power-producing rivers, our lumber, our minerals, our fisheries, our more fruitful agricultural areas had been taken under new management—private ownership. So that generation was forced to pause and find service before giant looms, fiery furnaces, great presses in buildings immense in size to those accustomed to gaze on log and sod houses and the various improvisations for shelter of the pioneering period.

The bulk of the people found themselves bound to this puzzling giant in return for crude food and shelter and rough comforts. They were to become its victims and its servants as though divinely ordained to this service. This New Industrialism was a giant and a very cruel master to those not used to his discipline. But as time passed, the new industrial order became the accepted order. It brought benefits on the whole, comforts and luxuries unknown to the pioneers, varied food, medical attention and an offer of education and intellectual pleasures.

That these benefits were not well diffused; that thousands perished because of long hours of enforced labor; that many sickened with the monotony of their toil and the laborious tasks they underwent, was lost sight of in the general acclaim for the *new industrialism*, which promised to bring competence to all.

It slowly dawned on the workers that while they were living on a hazardous level, their masters were accumulating wealth in dazzling amounts, to their simple reckoning. There were those who sought to better the conditions of themselves and their fellows.

They formed labor unions whose members and officers

were hounded by the police as foolish malcontents threatening public order. But slowly, with a more general recognition that industrial employment and its surroundings might immeasurably be bettered, the labor unions were allowed to foment their opinions and gather added membership. There had come a demarcation between the New Industrialism and the people, the line of cleavage being as to whether or not new forms in industry might not accomplish more for the body of the people.

It was at this period that Edward Bellamy's book, "Looking Backward," was printed (Houghton Mifflin Company in 1887), about fifty years ago. The story aroused the greatest controversy any book on social and economic matters has had. On two continents, America and Europe, the profoundest discussions followed its publication.

Bellamy cast the period of his book as of the year 2000. Its hero had been put into a hypnotic sleep in 1887 and had been awakened 113 years later to find that economic tendencies, which Bellamy titled "the economic revolution," had resulted in complete nationalization of industry, commerce and labor. All of the people served at tasks to which they were best adapted. The working hours were easy and the results, as measured in the ownership and use of material things, in freedom for social and intellectual pastime and in cultural betterments, were astounding.

Bellamy's philosophy was a gentle one. He did not ask that overnight the great industries and the daily paths of the people should be violated. He held instead, that the tendencies of industry and imposed economics

11

were toward a self-nationalization by consolidations and concentration of wealth and purpose; that each industry as it reached a status of ill was nationalized as a last resort as good public policy.

This philosophy, so different from the "let well enough alone" teachings of the early English economists, whose trend of thought found mere echo among their confrerees in the United States, was so revolutionary it stirred the intellectuals in economics of all civilized countries. For many years it was rare that any journal of opinion in either continent went to press without a defense of or an attack on the Bellamy philosophy. The Nationalists, a political party espousing Bellamy's doctrine, attracted hundreds of thousands of members.

Bellamy, the son of a Baptist minister, whose education had been obtained abroad and in extensive travel and observation in the United States, was an urbane, gentle creature, frail in body, who died in 1898, a few months after he had elaborated the views in "Looking Backward" in a volume titled "Equality" (D. Appleton-Century Company, 1936, original copyright, 1897).

Bellamy was a delighted and delightful antagonist for his economic foes. His writing style was unusually elevated, but his most lofty words always had feet. He neither dodged nor retreated before the great volleys poured on him. His books reached a sale of more than a million copies, so that all the intellectual and laboring world took part in what has been described as the greatest intellectual ferment the world has seen on any subject other than a religious one.

There have been great minds in the world who have

dreamed of Utopias and of Blessed Lands where brotherhood, fraternity and equality should reign. But
Bellamy not only created his world, but he also peopled
it. He supplied an answer to every valid objection made
to it. More, he set out in detail the government and the
economic and social order of his New Land in the
minutest particular.

He met savants on their ground and became a familiar
of labor. He labored by pen and speech for ten years
in one of the greatest intellectual battles this nation has
known with an endurance and resolve which strained
his slight physique. But he never seemed ruffled, never
angry and never perturbed while combatting every fact
and every reasoning that could be aligned against him.

The secret of the great sale of his books was not only
the novelty of the locale in which he placed "Looking
Backward" and its sequel, "Equality." It came in the
fact that he put "living" men and women, with human
likes and dislikes, preferences and prejudices, into economics. That dry and stale subject sparkled within its
living tissue. It became animate and readily intelli-
gible.

One species of attack leveled at Bellamy was that
he was a dreamer. This charge was given substance because long before the world had even dreamed of the
radio, television, aviation, motor cars and other modern
inventions which have mystified the people with their
arrival they were already provided in Bellamy's New
Land. He wrote of them as casually as would a writer
of today.

Everyone in the New Land had an equal income and

pleasant work, or if not, was compensated by shorter hours of labor. His people had time for companionship and the enjoyment of great books and dramas. The authors of these found compensation in exact relation to their merit, for they were given leisure to pursue their ambition only through the contribution of their readers and auditors, who would meet the cost of the authors' absence from productive labor by contribution from their store of national wealth.

There was no crime, there being no incentive for theft. Woman had gained social and economic independence in receiving the same compensation every other citizen received. There were, as a consequence, no marriages of convenience or necessity, wedlock being a love state.

The nation provided homes and work, great places of assemblage in educational and cultural pursuits and public dining, quick transportation and immediate intelligences. Newspapers existed, but only as they could coax subscribers in the way the authors did. The practitioners of medicine, of astronomy and of the various sciences gave their services nationally and for incomes equal to that of all others.

Agriculture had reached its zenith in health and comfort, for the tillers had every known luxury in food, and conveniences in home appliances, transportation and a closely-connected social life. Men and women workers took pride in tasks well done. Merit was fully rewarded by the public esteem in which the leaders in various departments of the national industry were held as they performed their tasks or completed the marvelous inventions of the age.

FOREWORD

The Bellamy philosophy was perfected at a time in which there was only dim public apprehension that a new social and economic epoch was being ushered in. And with it a thousand and one problems that have since urgently pressed for answers they have not fully received. The unanswered problems collided with irresistible unity and fury in the world collapse of 1929, which has remained to plague all civilized peoples.

It was then realized that similar forces, class antagonisms, hatreds, greed and an alarming disregard of future consequence were universal. Since, the nations have tried to solve their problems, each in its own way. In European and Asiatic countries, these efforts resulted in Fascism, Communism and Nazism, totalitarian in status. Their defects largely arise from the efforts of their dictators to remain in power by aligning industry with the state, the opposite of true democracy, instead of controlling or disarming it.

In the United States, the change was sought to be effected through the New Deal. The main weakness of the New Deal is that, radical and revolutionary as it appeared at its baptism, it is neither radical nor revolutionary enough to fully meet the needs of a democracy. It has been unable to check the Bellamy-predicted drift toward Nationalism. It cannot as long as the owners of concentrated wealth, operating in various mischievous ways and channels, do not heed the certain fact that their selfish use of seized power is piling up a head of public fury that must result in their capitulation and the institution of industry for use and not for profit.

That condition, of course, would be full-cousin to Na-

FOREWORD

tionalism. The New Deal provided the soft and generous way toward a lessening of public anger, rising still in bounding strides, against the spectacle of a democracy, dominated by monopolies, being forced to deny its people bread and the full enjoyment of the marvelous advances in science, chemistry and invention.

We have a civilization of sorts in the United States. We have been able to retrograde from the independence of pioneer days to the most vicious point in Roman civilization, with satraps of immense wealth defying their government and holding virtually sole dominion of life and death over millions, unyielding in their greed to the voice of patriotism and of reason and common sense.

This present volume is composed entirely of matter written by Bellamy in the 1891-1893 period. By that time the discussion had reached a practical stage. Various artisans, ministers and workers had asked Bellamy to enlarge on what part their vocations would play in the New Land he had created.

One chapter of the book, placed first, is extremely interesting as defining the differences between Nationalism, Communism and Socialism. For these articles, which Bellamy published in The New Nation, of which he was editor, the creator of the New Land used a style of phrasing new to him, compared with the elevated level of his books and in the discussions they aroused with economists and various intellectuals. They show the practicality of the Bellamy mind, however, and his readiness in adapting his philosophy to practical needs.

His thought is brought home at this time by reflection on the tendencies in industry and business apparent today. We find the railroads, which Bellamy said would first be nationalized, struggling feebly and it may be ineffectually against so-called government ownership, really nationalization. We find the utilities, which were named second among the great businesses whose conduct will lead to nationalism, showing symptoms of nationalization in the gradual growth of municipal plants and the "yardstick" of the federal government in the Tennessee Valley authority, with its plan to absorb in federal control power companies in a section of the Middle South.

We find our insurance companies so pregnable, they have twice appealed for government aid, once that Congress raise railroad rates to protect their investments and again a plea for loans to replenish their diminishing reserves and also that loans be made to industries in which they held investment securities.

Insurance was the third of the industries that would fall, Bellamy predicted. So that the entrance of the federal government in a limited way into that field in old-age insurance, unemployment insurance and other avenues makes this prediction acceptable.

Among the other great industries which reveal inward convulsions that threaten them as private enterprises is the widely-spread coal mining activities and the vast commercial empire built up in the distribution of this necessity. Progress toward nationalization of coal already is underway. The mine owners, their employees and the public are a unit in demanding that a durable peace be found for the many vexing problems which have arisen. The government has taken an unavailing

17

hand in the effort and already it is the consensus of many of the mine owners that the only solution to the problem is government purchase and operation.

Incidentally, the increasing amalgamations and consolidations in industry and banking, with absolute control of finances by the national government; the faster pulse toward restraint of corporations with monopolistic powers and the growing opposition to the patent laws as now constituted, the privileges of which annually take billions of dollars from the consumers, deprive thousands of opportunity in life and business and which, readily lending themselves to the imposition of prices which withhold the advances of science and progress from use by the great majority of the people, do much to give a hand to the move toward the nationalization of which Bellamy speaks.

Bellamy said that the rest of the world had followed America's example in the concepts on which the New Land had been established and that international trade was free and balanced by exchange of products of equal value between the nations. This, too, is approaching in the international reciprocal trade pacts supported by the efforts of Cordell Hull, secretary of state.

It is a commentary on human intelligence and a repellant one, that the greatest monopolies in the United States are based on governmental privilege, the patent and the tariff. An end to these privileges would hold back the growing sentiment toward nationalism and operation for service only, but it is doubtful if it would stop it. One may only speculate on this.

A vital growth over the world the last few decades,

which is just now affecting the United States materially, is that of consumers' cooperatives. The formation of a consumers' or a producers' cooperative is little else than fulfillment of an unconscious desire toward centralization or nationalism, whatever it may be termed. Security is the dominant wish of today and it will be gained either through present forms of government or through some improvisation which seems fitted to needs. In order to obtain some measure of it, people join whatever organization they feel will best promote their security.

Dream or possibility, whatever one may think of Bellamy's creation, it inspires, it fills the soul with an ineffable longing, it satisfies that very human quality of gentleness and will to service without which no one is complete.

Above all the evolution which has taken place since Bellamy died, none has the weight toward affirming belief in ultimate nationalization as does the present temper of the bulk of the American people. The great majorities given the New Deal, the continued faith in moves toward democratizing industry as politics has been democratized; the idea that industry and wealth are not ends in themselves, in that there are better ways in which the nations may live in peace and each share the products of their common effort, will not down.

These ideas, commonly ascribed to "public unrest" by the politicians and the other unthinking, root far deeper than any surface effect. They rise out of the World War. The public conscience unwittingly realizes that if billions may be spent without stint and human lives sacrificed without mercy in the name of patriotism, patriotism must have a sounder bottom than the one the war veterans returned to. What avail the war? they ask. What the profit?

They saw this nation nationalized for a supreme effort in bloody carnage. Their query is why not a nationalization for peace and security? The effort to have industry and business mobilized in war is the spirit of nationalization. They further want to know what security in life can they have when men in high places and the journalistic crews unite to stifle every decent ambition men of family have.

These are the very questions which Bellamy asked in his generation. Present conditions are such as those he believed would induce and give impetus to complete nationalization of every activity in the United States. Were Bellamy here today, it is certain there would be at least one man content in the thought that his individual philosophy not only lives but also thrives.

And he has 62 years, two full generations yet, to see his fruit blossom and bud and ripen from the seed he sowed!

"Men fight for crusts when they are starving, but they do not quarrel over bread at a banquet table. Somewhat so it befell when in the years after the Revolution material abundance and all the comforts of life came to be a matter of course for every one, and storing for the future was needless. Then it was that the hunger motive died out of human nature and covetousness as to material things, mocked to death by abundance, perished by atrophy, and the motives of the modern worker, the love of honor, the joy of beneficence, the delight of achievement, and the enthusiasm of humanity, became the impulses of the economic world." (Edward Bellamy in "Equality.")

II

The New Nation

Following is the prospectus which Edward Bellamy wrote as a notice of the establishment of The New Nation, of which he remained as editor during its life. In its columns, through argument for nationalism and counter blasts, which he used freely in The New Nation, Bellamy defined and refined the entire theory of his central philosophy, which afterwards was embraced in "Equality," his master work. The material following chapter 2 of this publication appeared in The New Nation.

THE New Nation will criticize the existing industrial system as radically wrong in morals and preposterous economically, and will advocate the substitution therefor, as rapidly as practicable, of the plan of national industrial co-operation, aiming to bring about the economic equality of citizens, which is known as nationalism.

It is intended to make the proposed periodical a newspaper of the industrial and social movement. There will be an attempt to present a summary, from week to week, of noteworthy facts and events in this and foreign countries, which illustrate the necessity, the tendencies, and the possibilities of industrial reform. It is believed that

21

facts are, today, the best advocates of nationalism. The tendencies of business are arguments to which its most stubborn opponents can make no reply.

. . . .

There will be an attempt to educate the public to an intelligent understanding of its claims; to be regarded in its immediate application as the only possible escape from plutocracy, and as promising in its ultimate results an industrial order which, while far more efficient than the present system in the production of wealth, shall by the manner of its distribution satisfy the heart and conscience of man.

Prominence will be given to the fact that nationalism is pre-eminently the cause of woman, because it alone, among all doctrines of social reform, recognizes that the burden she bears for the race is a title to the human heritage and to its product as sacred as that of toil.

In hearty recognition that the Christian churches and other religious bodies are awakening to the fact that an industrial system based upon the principles of human brotherhood is nothing more than the practical application of the essential principles of religion and the express teachings of Christ, The New Nation will give prominence to utterances of the pulpit and religious press, which indicates a sympathy with industrial reform, and will welcome discussions of social problems from a religious standpoint.

As first steps toward nationalism, The New Nation will advocate civil-service reform in a more radical form than it has been commonly urged heretofore, and will propose the organization of all bodies of public employees upon a basis of guaranteed rights, absolutely preventing executive interference with individuals for political purposes. The New Nation will advocate the immediate nationalization of the telegraph, telephone and express service, of the railroad system, and of the coal mines of the country. It will advocate the assumption by municipalities of all public services now performed by corporations, and of any other businesses which may be advantageously conducted in the public interest. The New Nation will also advocate the equalization of educational opportunities as between rich and poor, and generally speaking will support all reforms tending to humaner, more fraternal and more equal conditions in society.

The New Nation will diligently seek to promote a closer union between the various reform bodies and industrial organizations, both of artisans and farmers, with the purpose of bringing their combined influence to bear for the procurement of legislation as to reforms upon the necessity of which they agree.

. . . .

While naturally counting on the sympathy of persons already convinced of the necessity of radical reform, it is hoped that The New Nation will prove to be a paper which will not need to depend for its support upon the sympathy of its audience; but will be found valuable, not only to those who wish well to its cause, but to all who desire to keep informed upon the present worldwide movement for a new and better social order, whether they sympathize with it or not.

January 31, 1891.　　　EDWARD BELLAMY, Editor.

III

Talks on Nationalism—To a Seeker of Definitions

Mr. Smith, who has joined the nationalists, meets a seeker after definitions, who wants to have him define exactly the difference between Communism, Socialism and Nationalism.

Seeker of Definitions:– Look here, Smith, what do you call yourselves?

Smith:– Nationalists.

Seeker of Definitions:– Yes, I know; but just what does that mean? Does it really mean anything new? The world is so full of words that people have no business to coin a new one unless it is necessary. I see that many critics declare that Nationalism is nothing but Communism.

Smith:– Yes, I perceive that some have taken that method of advertising their ignorance. It serves the purpose very well.

Seeker of Definitions:– There are others who declare that nationalism is all one with socialism. What do you say to that?

Smith:– Simply that socialism has become a term too broad and inclusive to serve any longer as a specific

24

definition. In its dictionary sense, it stands for any theory which advocates a more orderly, just and harmonious arrangement of society. In that sense, it includes all schools of radical social reformers, and among them nationalists. With that understanding nationalists may be properly called socialists, but not when speaking specifically, for the reason that among the many schools of reform which claim the name of socialists, there are some which differ broadly from nationalists. To use the same term for groups so different in aims only produces confusion.

Seeker of Definitions:— I have heard it said that all theories of radical industrial and social reorganization are properly to be classed under one or the other of two formulas. One is that of the communists: "From each according to his abilities; to each according to his needs." The other is the formula of socialism: "To each according to his deeds,"—that is, I suppose, the amount of his actual performance. Now, which of those formulas does nationalism come under?

Smith:— Neither the first nor the second, but under a third and wholly different one, namely: "From each equally; to each equally." The ridiculous notion about there being only two possible formulas to be followed in industrial reconstruction is, I judge, the real explanation of the misconstructions of nationalism which you refer to.

Seeker of Definitions:— Then I understand that you reject the communistic formula?

Smith:— As a practical rule for an industrial system, yes; morally speaking, no. Every good man has always

25

recognized that the measure of his due service to humanity is his ability, and that the appeal of need is sacred to all he has. That formula must always be the ethical standard for the individual. But any law of service or distribution must proceed by fixed and obvious standards, and what a person's potential abilities may be, or what his real needs are, as compared with those of others, neither he nor anyone else can tell. In religious communities, and other groups specially constituted, the determination of duty and of need has been successfully left to the individual conscience, and possibly in some quite ideal conditions of universal moral refinement, this might be safely done in the community at large; but for any present purposes the communistic formula is obviously impracticable.

Seeker of Definitions:– What have you to say to the socialist formula. "To each according to his deeds"?

Smith:– That is just as impracticable as the other.

Seeker of Definitions:– I don't see why it isn't practicable enough. What does it amount to except giving to each man what he earns?

Smith:– If that is all, how does it differ from the present system?

Seeker of Definitions:– Because under the present system the workers do not have equal opportunities. As I understand it the socialist formula means "a fair field and no favor and let the best man win."

Smith:– "And the devil take the hindmost." It appears to me that the formula as you explain it, merely means a more strictly scientific and pitiless application of the principle which too largely animates the present sys-

26

tem, namely, that might makes right, and that men's only duties are to themselves. It is proposed to make the conditions of the struggle fairer as between the strong, but the weak are to be even worse off than now, for the laws which at present to some extent secure their claims upon stronger individuals and upon the state, would be repugnant to the strict application of the principle "to each according to his deeds." The order of things which would follow the logical enforcement of this maxim, would be far more favorable to cruelty and oppression than even that which now exists. It is called, I know, the socialist formula, but in my opinion it does injustice to the sentiments of a large proportion of the socialists, and fully represents only the anarchist wing of that diversified body.

Seeker of Definitions:– Well, but admitting that the maxim is rather hard on the weaklings, isn't it after all, justice?

Smith:– On the contrary, a law awarding to each the value of his deeds or work, as a matter of absolute right would be fradulent, because it would assume that an individual owns himself and has a valid title to the full usufruct of his powers without incumbrance or obligation on account of his debt to the past and his duties toward the social organism of which he is a part and by virtue of which only he is able to work more effectually than a savage. This assumption is wholly false. "No man liveth to himself." The powers he has inherited from the common ancestry of the race measure his debt to his contemporaries, not his claims upon them. The strong

27

are the rightful servants and debtors of the weak, not their masters.

Seeker of Definitions:– Well, I'm bound to admit that you have pretty good moral authority for that proposition even if it does seem a little startling. But allowing all you say about the moral quality of the maxim, "to each according to his deeds," it does not follow that it is impracticable. Very immoral things are sometimes unluckily quite practicable.

Smith:– This is not one of them. The proposition to base the industrial system upon distributing to every one according to his deeds, assumes that it is possible in some logical and generally acceptable manner to settle the absolute value in comparison with one another of the hundreds of kinds of work, of brain and mind and heart, which contribute to the well-being of human society. There are only two ways in which any settlement of this thousand-fold question can be made. One is by the haggling of the market place, each worker or group of workers taking the best advantage he can of the needs of the others. The other is, by arbitrary edict of the state. If the relative value of services is to be determined by the market place, we have not advanced one step beyond the present system. The shylock, the cornerer, the engrosser, the regrater, whether acting for himself or as the agent of a group of workers, will find himself as much at home and prosper as greatly as to-day. "Old Hutch" if he lives, will find steady employment as selling agent for farmers, and Jay Gould will command his own terms for his services in marketing at a good price the coal product for the miners. On the other hand, if any government undertook by arbitrary edict to fix the comparative value of all sorts of work and service, who is sanguine enough to suppose that it would survive the discontents of the first pay-day? No; the maxim, "to each according to his deeds," is not only cruel but fraudulent, and not only cruel and fraudulent, but likewise impracticable.

Seeker of Definitions:– Well, now let us pick a few flaws in your nationalist maxim "from each equally to each equally." Where do you get that idea from? Why should we regard that as any more practicable than the other, till it has been tried?

Smith:– It has been tried and is being tried all over the world. It is as old in its root as the idea of the nation, and has developed in clearness and breadth of application with the evolution of the nation. It is the idea that the relation of the nation with all its members should be an equal one as to all mutual obligations. "From all equally to all equally" is to-day the fundamental idea of all public regulations and policies in all progressive modern states. Exceptions here and there still exist but they are fast-decaying relics of old abuses. There is to-day one law as to taxation, one as to military service, one as to judicial liability, and one as to all other duties of the people toward the nation. Reciprocally, the nation recognizes an equal duty toward all citizens. It is no respecter of persons, and wherever there is an exception to that rule it is recognized as an abuse to be reformed. We nationalists so call ourselves because we propose to extend the national organization, which has hitherto been limited to the political, judicial and military aspects of

29

the state, to its industries also. This step necessarily implies that under the proposed national industrial system, the nation should be no respecter of persons in its industrial relations with its members, but that the law should be, as already in its political, judicial and military organization, "From all equally; to all equally."

Seeker of Definitions:– But that, as applied to industry, is nonsense. People will not be capable of the same industrial service.

Smith:– No more are they capable of the same military service, no more are they capable of equal political intelligence, no more do they pay equal taxes; nevertheless, they are equally protected by the army, the fleet and the courts, and their votes weigh equally in settling the destinies of the nation. The demand of the nation upon all is equal, but where there is inability, either partial or complete to fulfill the demand, the nation does not, therefore, diminish its service of protection toward the citizen. The army fights for him though he cannot fight, and the taxes are spent for him though he can pay none. It is not possible that any other law should prevail under a national organization of industry. There will be an equal law of service for all and an equal provision for all, but inability, complete or partial to render the service, will not have any effect to diminish the provision. Nationalism is not, as silly people have imagined, a fanciful theory, which either may or may not have any foundation. It is based upon the logic and doctrine of the nation, and merely predicts the next and a very near step in the evolution of its fundamental idea.

IV

Talks on Nationalism—To an Investment Banker

Mr. Smith, who has joined the nationalists, meets a nationalist who is an Investment Banker. They discuss the bearing of nationalism upon investments.

Smith:– How is the investment business, nowadays?

Investment Banker:– As bad as possible. I've been in it 30 years, but I never had so much difficulty in advising people where to invest money as I am having now. Of course, there are plenty of enterprises which would be glad to take all they could get, but I'm not looking out merely for my commission; I have a little reputation as a careful adviser which I want to keep, even if I lose some money.

Smith:– Then I take it you don't recommend railroad securities.

Investment Banker:– There are some which everybody knows are sound, but of course everybody knows also that the railroad business in this country is in a condition of corruption and chaos, which makes the securities of the majority of lines purely speculative investments. I don't deal in them.

Smith:– According to your notion, what is the matter with the railroad system?

Investment Banker:– General cussedness; a hopeless complication of bad morals and crazy economics.

Smith:– Do you think that the decline in railroad securities is pretty near at an end?

Investment Banker:– By no means! The end isn't in sight. The decline will not touch bottom till every water dollar has been squeezed out of the goods. Then the government will step in and take them at their actual valuation; for, of course, anybody is bound to see that government ownership of the railroad system is the only possible logical or proper outcome of the present intolerable situation. Talking about the decline in railroad securities now going on, this same prospect of government purchase, which is looming up bigger and plainer every day, is a very good reason itself for predicting that the decline will continue till the true value is reached, because it is certain that when the government takes the roads, it will not pay more than their actual valuation.

Smith:– I should think that, as a government ownership man, you would find yourself rather lonesome among the financiers.

Investment Banker:– Don't suppose any such thing. No honest banker or broker has any desire to deal in securities which, like those of our railroads at present, are nothing but the marked cards of professional gamblers. Let the government buy the roads, and we shall have, in place of these devices of fraud, national bonds at two per cent; and then we and our customers will know where we stand. The change will not only be an enormous gain to the people at large, but will steady the whole financial world.

Smith:— Does not the same argument apply generally in favor of national and municipal purchases of telegraph lines, express companies, street-lighting plants and street railroad systems? There are very few of these concerns which are not at present greatly over-capitalized, and their securities consequently either unstable, or likely to be so, if the truth were known. Would it not be a boon to the investing public, as well as to the people at large, if all these concerns were bought out at actual valuation by the government, and public bonds at low rate of interest took their place?

Investment Banker:— Certainly; the same argument applies to all these classes of investments. I never recommend a customer to invest in telegraph, street car or any of those lines of securities without finding out whether they are over-capitalized; for, as surely as public ownership of such service is coming, their securities will, in the end, be scaled down to actual valuation.

Smith:— What do you say about the stock of the big manufacturing trusts, the "industrials," as investments?

Investment Banker:— The operations of the sugar trust have given a black eye to that sort of security. No doubt some of them are good, if one could know the inside situation, but, as a rule, they are speculative, and the man who loses by investing in them can't expect much sympathy.

Smith:– I observe, of late, that the craze for stocking industrial and commercial business is spreading at such a rate among the smaller concerns that we shall soon be able to buy shares in peanut stands and barber shops.

Investment Banker:– Yes, and it is a mighty unhealthy sign, too. Some of these investments are doubtless sound, but in many cases I judge they are speculative, or mere devices to make a profitable disposition of a declining business. I see that in some instances the employees are "permitted" to take stock. As a rule, I would advise them to take good advice before availing themselves of the "permission." When they have taken stock their employers have a hold on them they did not have before, while on the other hand, being in a minority as stockholders, they are as powerless as ever as to the management.

Smith:– But what do you let your customers invest in? Supposing a man, through no fault of his own, has a little money, what are you going to let him do with it, pending the arrival of the good time coming? Must he bury it in the ground? How about real estate?

Investment Banker:– I have no objection to that. It is certainly safer than any of the investments we have mentioned. But my chief line is public bonds, national and municipal. I believe they are the coming security. As public ownership and control through the purchase of private plants extends over one branch of business after another, national and municipal bonds will take the place of the stocks and bonds of private companies and corporations until there are no other securities in the market.

Smith:— But they will not be permanent. They will be in constant course of extinguishment by the operation of sinking funds, till finally there are none left, and the nation owns the entire national estate and complete machinery of production in fee absolute.

Investment Banker:— Precisely; the progress of nationalism will of course eventually put an end to the investment business altogether by putting an end to the interest system and dispensing with the private capitalist entirely. I only say that national and municipal bonds will survive longer than any other form of securities, and are therefore, in my opinion, the best.

Smith:— So far as I understand you, then, there is nothing in the programme of nationalism that need cause any panic among financiers.

Investment Banker:— Nothing at all, I am sure. The advent of nationalism means, indeed, a judgment day sooner or later for all false values and fraudulently inflated enterprises, for the nation will not pay for water, but otherwise the expectation of nationalism, will, by the justice of its method and the clearness and certainty of its evolution, have a steadying effect on the general market. As a financier, I confess, indeed, to a certain scientific pleasure in contemplating the exceedingly simple and logical character of the nationalist programme in its financial aspect. The first phase will be the gradual substitution, at a rate of interest necessarily ruling ever lower, of public for private securities, as the process of public acquisition goes on. Two noticeable features will characterize this phase. In the first place, in proportion as business becomes public, with the public credit behind it, it will become steadied, and panics and crises will be diminished, a result further contributed to by the non-fluctuating value of the public bonds which will more and more take the place of the securities of the bought-out private corporations. The other feature will be the diminishing value of money to its possessors, owing to the constantly narrowing field for its employment and the declining rate of interest. Meanwhile, however, as this process goes on, the extension of public employment with constantly enlarging guarantees as to maintenance to the employed and the dependent, will be gradually substituting a national pledge of security for a precarious dependence upon private hoards. The second phase of the transformation will consist in the progressive extinction, by the sinking funds, of the principal of the public debt. Long before that process has been completed, it is my opinion that the owners of public securities will largely waive their claims, for in proportion as the public monopoly of business has progressed, their money will not only have been deprived of earning power, but in proportion as the national organization for employment and maintenance is completed, of its buying power also. Money may still retain nominally its former legal-tender power for debts, but there will be no debts, nor any buying or selling among citizens; nor will men longer be able to buy services of one another. The nation will be sole employer and sole producer, and to the nation all must go for the supply of their needs. But citizenship will be the only basis of demand which the nation recognizes; money will be of no use or even meaning in negotiations to obtain so much as a loaf of bread from the nation; nor on the other hand will a ton of gold be accepted in lieu of the performance of the least duty which the citizen, under the equal law of service, owes the nation.

Smith:– You have figured down the evolution to the last link in the chain, but I suppose we shall agree that as soon as the people become fully conscious of the new order toward which they are moving, and begin to appreciate its advantages, the consummation is likely to be greatly accelerated by some general action taken with common consent. The first steps in the movement, its educational stage, will, no doubt, prove to have been the slowest and most difficult.

V

Talks on Nationalism—To a Public Speaker

Mr. Smith, who has lately joined the nationalists, meets a Public Speaker, who has just delivered a lecture entitled "Nationalism vs. Individuality."

Public Speaker:– How are you, Smith? By the way, did you see the account of my lecture in the papers this morning?

Smith:– Yes; I read it.

Public Speaker:– What did you think of it? Of course, I don't suppose you liked it.

Smith:– To tell the truth, I was very much surprised by it.

Public Speaker:– Why surprised? You didn't suppose I was a nationalist, did you?

Smith:– No; it wasn't that. What surprised me was, that you should pick out the point of the nationalist system to attack which you did. I was surprised in very much the same way a general might be to see an adversary select the strongest point of his position to assault.

Public Speaker:– It seems to me the weakest, and at least you will admit that I'm not alone in that opinion.

38

TO A PUBLIC SPEAKER

It is the criticism most commonly passed upon nationalism that it would tend to destroy individuality.

Smith:— Yes, I know it. The fact is not difficult to account for, however. Nationalism has come so suddenly to the front that it caught the political economists unprepared. All the ammunition they had available consisted of the forty-year-old arguments against Fourierism and Cabetism, which were none too applicable even to those systems, and utterly fail to hit nationalism at all. After a while no doubt they will discover that they somehow have not got the range, and then it is possible they may think it worth their while to manufacture some relevant arguments.

Public Speaker:— Then it is your opinion that nationalism is not opposed to individuality?

Smith:— It is not a matter of opinion, but of examination.

Public Speaker:— Which means, I suppose, that I have not examined the subject. Well, perhaps I have not. Perhaps I am attacking the strongest point of nationalism. If so, it ought to be easy to defend it. What have you got to say against this notion, which, right or wrong, so many people seem to share, that nationalism is opposed to individuality?

Smith:— Why, simply that the whole system of nationalism is necessarily, by its essential principle, committed to encouraging the utmost possible development of the individuality of every person in the nation, as the only means of getting the most and best service out of him. Does a wise farmer hitch thoroughbreds to the plough or put the plough-horse into the sulky? That is the way the present industrial system misuses men and wastes their forces, because in it there is no idea of a commonwealth or any general economy of forces for the behoof of all; but nationalism being expressly a plan for economizing the forces of all the people for the greatest possible result, in which all are to share, is pledged by its very principle to see that every one's special faculties and aptitudes are cultivated, and when ascertained are given the utmost scope. Don't you see how evident it is that the development of individuality, instead of being hindered by nationalism, is bound to be encouraged by it as an essential condition of the economical success of the system?

Public Speaker:– That view is not without some plausibility.

Smith:– Plausibility! Why, man, there isn't any other view that anybody but a blind man can take. In the first place, to the end of enabling people to find out what is in them, what their individuality really is, everybody, instead of a small minority of the people as now, willl receive the best possible education. It will next be the care of the nation to see that every man and woman has that career opened to him or her, out of the whole range of arts, trades and professions, which they choose and show themselves best fitted for. It will not be then, as now, a matter of luck, chance of influential friends and wealthy backing, to obtain entrance into the line of life-work one longs for, but it will be the policy of the nation, in the people's common interest, to see that merit alone commands precedence, and that the tools go always to the hands that best can use them. Where did you

40

pick up your notions about nationalism, anyhow? Certainly, you can never have read any of our literature.

Public Speaker:– I don't know what you call your literature. I have read a number of accounts of nationalism by our leading political economists. They ought to know what it is.

Smith:– They ought to know, certainly, and it is just possible that they do know, but no one would suspect it from the writings of many of them. The complaint against nationalism for its alleged tendency to discourage individuality is indeed one of the most striking illustrations of forgetting the beam in one's own eye in zeal to point out a mote in another's, that are on record. Not only does the present system deprive all but a privileged few, in the first place, of education enough to find out what they can do, and then interpose all possible obstacles to their getting a chance to do that, but worse still, its whole tendency is, by means of the economical pressure brought to bear upon everybody, to turn men and women into cowards and hypocrites, and make them lead false and double lives. At present, with few exceptions, from the rector in his pulpit to the street sweeper, we all depend for our maintenance upon the patronage of individuals or groups, and for our own sakes and the sake of our families we are constrained to be careful, in our walk and conversation, not to offend those on whom we depend for a living. There are certain politics it is well for us to profess, a certain church it is prudent to attend, and certain predjudices it is wise not to offend. So we are all enslaved together under a sordid mutual bondage one to another, from the least to the greatest, and only brave men dare show any individuality. Under nationalism, nobody, man or woman, will depend for support upon any other or group of others, but his account for duty and maintenance will be directly with the nation. It will be a feeble soul indeed which will not develop individuality then.

Public Speaker:– You have the advantage of me on that argument. I suppose you know it was by professing the wrong politics that I lost my place in ——'s last year.

Smith:– I did not know that, but it is pretty safe to assume that the argument is one which will touch a sore spot in the history of nine out of any ten men you may meet. I should think, I must say, that your experience would make you think favorably of nationalism, instead of setting you to lecturing against it.

Public Speaker:– Well, I'm going to revise that lecture on one or two points before I deliver it again.

VI

Talks on Nationalism—To a Lover of Freedom

Mr. Smith, who has recently joined the nationalist club, meets a lover of freedom, who, having read Herbert Spencer's "Coming Slavery," and other individualistic papers, fears that nationalism would result in a new despotism.

Lover of Freedom:— I concede the great efficiency of your proposed national cooperative plan of industry. By saving the wastes of competition, planlessness, idleness and business disturbances, it would, without question, vastly increase the industrial product of the world, and perhaps render possible the universal diffusion of comfort, if not of luxury; but there is a price too great to pay even for universal comfort, and that is freedom.

Smith:— Ah, then you share Herbert Spencer's apprehension?

Lover of Freedom:— I do. I fully believe that such a centralized industrial organization of the entire population as you propose would lead to a despotism such as the world never saw, and only to be compared with that which the Incas set up in ancient Peru.

Smith:— Yes, that is what Spencer says. I really think, though, that he must have been napping when he made that comparison. It is usually admitted that like re-sults follow only from like conditions, but anything more utterly different than the conditions which led to the Inca empire, and the social, democratic and nationalist movement of today, it would be impossible to imagine. The Inca system was imposed by a caste of nobles of reputed heavenly origin upon an inferior race; while na-tionalism, if established at all, will be the very consum-mation of democracy.

Lover of Freedom:— Nevertheless, despotism may be evolved from it. The officers of your state will find ways of perpetuating themselves in power, and, when once they get control of the industrial system, the very strength and perfection of the organization will make it the more efficient as an engine for overthrowing the liberty of the people.

Smith:— Whom are these officers going to get to help them to overthrow the people's liberties?

Lover of Freedom:— Ambitious men have never failed to find others to be their tools.

Smith:— They have never failed to find such tools because there has always been in every form of society, hitherto, a degraded class, ignorant, brutalized, and without any stake in the country, which it was easy to stir up against the intelligent and well-to-do supporters of the existing order. Without the assist-ance of such a proletariat class, no usurper, or band of usurpers, would ever have been able to revolutionize a state. Under nationalism, there will be no such class to appeal to. There will be no classes. There will be no portion of the community more ignorant or degraded than another. All will have the same stake in the existing condition of things, and the same interest in resisting any attempt to overthrow it.

Lover of Freedom:– There is a point there, I admit.

Smith:– I think you will have to admit that it is a complete answer to the prediction that any class will be able to establish a despotism upon the basis of nationalism. By the rule of absolute equality in the enjoyment of the social organization which nationalism establishes, it gives the state the broadest possible basis, and imparts a consequent stability to the structure greater than any social fabric ever before possessed.

Lover of Freedom:– There may be other sorts of oppression than subjection to an individual tyrant or an oligarchy. I grant that it would be rather difficult for an individual or a class despotism to establish itself under your system, but the very system itself is one of despotism. For the sake of the advantages of co-operation, each individual practically surrenders his liberties to the whole, and becomes part of a great industrial machine.

Smith:– Well, aren't we parts of a great industrial machine now. The only difference is that the present machine is a bungling and misconstructed one, which grinds up the bodies and souls of those who work in it, and turns out poverty, prostitution, insanity and suicide as its finished products, while the new machine will be scientifically constructed, with an equal view to the comfort of the workers and the increase of the product.

Lover of Freedom:– That the new machine is more scientifically constructed than the old I admit, but all its advantages would be more than offset, to a lover of freedom like myself, by the fact that I should be compelled to work in it, whereas now I can work or not, as I choose.

Smith:– That is to say, you can work, steal or starve. You have to take your choice between those three alternatives. There isn't any fourth one. Nationalism cuts off the last two. It will not permit a man either to steal or starve. What a horrible tyranny to be sure! See here, you are a busy man and always have been since I knew you. Do you like a loafer?

Lover of Freedom:– Can't say that I do.

Smith:– Well, then, why are you so anxious to provide for that class? It seems to me that any man born into this world, which has been prepared for his living by the toil, the sacrifices, the martyrdoms of innumerable ages of men and women, who proposes to enjoy all this as well as the labor of his contemporaries without contributing his part to preserve and transmit the heritage, ought to be ducked in a horse-pond.

Lover of Freedom:– You misunderstand. It is not that we individualists personally want to loaf. It is the principle of the thing we stick out for. We demand the right to loaf if we wish. The idea of compulsion is what we resent.

Smith:– Precisely. Well, it is just the principle we stick out for, too. No man has a right to loaf, if it is

TO A LOVER OF FREEDOM

meant by that a right to refuse a reasonable amount of service, because such refusal will necessarily make him a burden on the community, and the community has a right to provide against that. The complexity of the present system of industrial relations may prevent it from being always obvious that the man who does not work, lives upon other people's work, but under nationalism the fact will be always plain, and the would-be loafer will be regarded as a would-be thief. Always excepting this precious liberty of loafing, I am quite unable to understand what liberties the nationalist plan of industrial organization curtails. Assuming that it is right to require a man to work, is it a loss of liberty to guarantee him the opportunity to work at what he likes best and can do best? Is it tyranny to insure him promotion, leadership and honor in precise proportion to his achievement? Is it a curtailment of his liberty to make him absolutely free of dependence upon the favor of any individual or community for his livelihood by giving him the constitutional pledge of the nation for it? Is it oppressive to guarantee him against loss of income in old age, and absolute security as to the welfare of his wife and children after he is gone? If to do all these things for a man means to take away his liberties and tyrannize over him, we had better get a new dictionary, for the definitions in the old ones are evidently all wrong.

VII

Talks on Nationalism—To a Farmer

*Mr. Smith, who has joined the nationalists,
meets a friend, who is a farmer, and they
discuss some of the bearings of nationalism
upon agriculture.*

Smith:– That's a fine boy of yours. I saw him the
other day. Going to make a farmer of him?

Farmer:– No use to try; he won't hear of it. He
doesn't know exactly what it is he wants to do, but he
is mighty sure it isn't farming.

Smith:– What does he find against it?

Farmer:– Well, he is rather high-spirited to begin
with, and when I sent him into ——— to the high school,
he said the other scholars looked down on him because
he was a farmer's son.

Smith:– Was it so?

Farmer:– I guess it was. Do you ever see the funny
papers,—the illustrated ones, I mean, and the funny sto-
ries in the joke columns of the daily papers? It is the
farmer they make the butt, you know, most generally.
And my boy says, too, it's so in theaters. "Old Hay-
seed" is trotted out to make them laugh. Well, I'm too
old to care about it, but I know what the boy says is true.
It's hard work farming, but the boy's sturdy and no shirk.

TO A FARMER

It isn't the work he's afraid of but he can't stand being kind of made fun of and despised, as he says the farmer always is by the rest of the community. I tell him about the big men who have been farmers' sons, but he says it was the farmers' sons' every time and not the farmers, and that the only way they came to anything was by leaving farming when they were boys.

Smith:— A very clever boy.

Farmer:— You agree with him then?

Smith:— Farming, land tilling, call it what you will, is, according to my notion, the most joyous, manly, philosophically satisfactory and, in fact, the one wholly ideal way of living; but it is also true that as a matter of fact the farmer leads a dog's life and always has.

Farmer:— That's what my boy says. He says that he has picked up from the histories that in all ages of the world the tiller of the soil has been the lowest class in the social scale. He says that when all work was done by slaves, the lowest and worst treated were those who worked the soil, and that when slavery disappeared in Europe it disappeared first in the towns and among the commercial classes, and lingered last in the rural regions and among the agricultural occupations.

Smith:— Undoubtedly that is true. Even at the present time, when slavery has disappeared from Europe, the word peasant still distinguishes the agricultural worker as a lower, ruder, more ignorant and less civilized class than any other sort of workers. The word is, indeed, a synonym for loutishness and stupidity, the lowest town servant despising the peasant.

Farmer:— My boy says that in spite of all the fine

things which have been said about the American farmer, the tendency of things is to reduce him to the position the tiller of the soil has always occupied, and that if other boys want to go into farming with that prospect they may; he won't.

Smith:– From the way the farmers' boys are streaming into the towns it looks very much as if your boy spoke the mind of most of them.

Farmer:– Well, now why is it? Can you tell me what it is about farming which should have always made agriculturists the hardest worked, worst used, and most contemptuously treated class in the community?

Smith:– I can give you several pretty good reasons, at least. There are a number of respects in which the conditions of agriculture differ from those of any other and all other sorts of work. In the first place the farmer must live back in the thinly-settled districts, while the schools, churches, libraries and theatres cluster about the towns. As a result of this fact he suffers great loss of educational and social facilities as compared with other workers. This puts him at a great disadvantage with others in all competition or association. This same isolation of position, while separating him from other sorts of workers, makes combinations with his fellows for any form of united action very difficult, thus making him politically helpless as compared with other classes. Another very important difference between farming and other work is that while other workers may fix by combinations, laws or customs the amount and conditions of their labor, the farmer cannot control the amount or conditions of his task.

TO A FARMER

Nature is his task-master, and the necessity of keeping step with her throws him out of step with all other sorts of industry. This nature-conditioned character of his work is the cause, not only of the greatest hardships of the farmer, but of the great difficulties in organizing his industry as others are organized for economy of force. There are also economical characteristics of agriculture which strongly differentiate it from other businesses. The agriculturist cannot control his product as other workers control theirs. The impossibility of doing is twofold; first, on account of the vast number of those engaged independently in the business, but still more on account of the fact that the amount of the product, even if the producers could be combined, depends wholly on the caprice of nature. The farmer's calling is, in fact, as speculative as that of the grain broker who preys on him. This fact greatly increases the difficulty of carrrying into agriculture the system which enables men to master their business instead of being mastered by it. These will serve, perhaps, as a few of the reasons which account for the depressed condition of agriculture in all ages. It has been assumed by superficial observers that in this country a new era of dignity and prosperity for the farmer had opened up, but that is not so. The first couple of centuries or so after this country's settlement were, indeed, a golden age for agriculture, but only on account of the special and transient conditions of a new country, which will not appear again till another virgin continent shall be discovered. This golden age was at an end a generation ago for the eastern farmer, and is now at an end for the westerner. With the filling up

51

of this country and the growth of commercial and manufacturing classes the farmer is finding himself as ever
before in history, the under dog in the fight for existence. The only thing that can prevent our agricultural
population from lapsing into the condition of peasantry
within a couple of generations is a radical transformation
in the conditions of agriculture.

Farmer:– Like what?

Smith:– Like that which nationalism proposes.

Farmer:– I have heard a good deal about nationalism,
but I'm not quite sure I know just what it means, especially as regards the farming business.

Smith:– It means the plan for carrying on all the
industries of the country by the nation for the general
interest, instead of leaving them to be carried on as now
by particular people for their particular interests. The
first result would be to equalize the burden of different
sorts of labor, and the conditions of life for different
classes of workers. As the work of the farmers is at
present vastly harder than anybody else's, and the conditions of his life are ruder and more disagreeable than
those of any other class, he would be a greater gainer than
any other class by the change, wouldn't he?

Farmer:– I don't see why, as things are now, he
wouldn't be bound to be a gainer by any sort of evening
up arrangement.

Smith:– Take, for instance, the modern movement
for a reduction of workingmen's hours. Few classes of
workers in towns now labor over 10 hours a day, many
only nine, while some have reduced the time to eight, and
all expect to succeed in doing so. Meanwhile the farmer

works as hard and as long as his physical strength will possibly endure, and sees no way of lessening his task unless he would fall hopelessly behind his fellows and forfeit his living. Now nationalism while requiring work of every citizen, would leave it to him to elect the sort he would do, and it is plain that in order to secure any farmers it would be necessary to make farm work as attractive as any other. The rule instead of being now, the harder the work the more the hours, would be the exact reverse, and it is probable that the farm worker's day instead of being the longest of all would be one of the shortest of labor days, especially in the severe heats of summer.

Farmer:– It is plain you don't know much about farming. All the Congresses in the world couldn't fix the length of the farmer's day in the planting or harvest season. He must keep up with the crops or lose them.

Smith:– Of course, and even though he should work 24 hours out of the 24, the farmer cannot keep up with nature. Under the co-operative system of nationalism, however, it will be perfectly feasible to keep up with the crops without working any man over the six or eight hours that may be the fixed labor day. It will be possible then, and indeed necessary, in order to secure the farmer a limited day's work, to provide for relays of men, day and night shifts if necessary, as is the practice in other businesses when there is a press of work. Until this principle of relays is introduced, it will be impossible to shorten or fix in any way the farmer's day's work, and this principle cannot be introduced until something like nationalism is established.

Farmer:– If you can make that out you will make a strong bid for the farmer's support.

Smith:– I don't think it is necessary to make it out. The statement is self-evident. The fact is, as you said, that no law can lessen or fix a farmer's hours of labor as it can other workers', because he must keep pace with nature. But while the amount of work necessary on a given piece of land in a given time cannot be fixed by any system, it is possible by a system to provide such a force of men as shall prevent the inexorable necessity of keeping pace with the operations of nature from crushing any individual or set of individuals. Some system of co-operation, therefore, with resources large enough to enable a force to be supplied which shall always equal the varying demand of the seasons is essential, if the farmer is ever to be as well off as other workers.

Farmer:– I guess that's about so, but may not some form of co-operation answer the purpose which shall be less than the complete plan of national co-operation you propose; some form of co-operation, for instance, limited to the farmers themselves?

Smith:– Such sorts of co-operation, limited to people of the same occupation are useful as stepping-stones to nationalism, and in this sense we nationalists hail all these partial applications of the idea of a commonwealth and a mutual dependence, but in no occupation will they furnish more than a very feeble suggestion of the advantages of complete national co-operation, and this is particularly so in farming. In various ways co-operation will help the farmers, and is in every way to be encouraged, but, unless national, it would do little to lighten the burden of labor by securing regular and reasonable hours of labor for the reason that when the farmers of a given district are idle they are all idle, and when they are busy they are too busy to help one another. If the farmer is to be helped out in this particular it can only be by the resources of national co-operation.

Farmer:– But how are farmers to be helped out by men who are not farmers?

Smith:– Perhaps, to some extent as they are now in the harvest season, by comparatively unskilled labor, but while the extra harvest labor now consists of worthless vagabonds who have idled away the rest of the year, it would under nationalism consist of detachments from the national industrial force under proper discipline and accustomed to be directed upon the shortest notice upon one point or another of the general field of industry as occasion arose.

Farmer:– Well, it would be very pleasant not to have to work over eight hours a day in harvest season, that's a fact, but there's another side to it. If we farmers work too hard in summer it's only honest to say that we don't work hard enough in winter, unless, you know, we happen to have a wood lot or a milk route. I'm afraid you'd be puzzled to provide us in all cases a good eight hours' work every day of winter.

Smith:– You touch on one of the greatest economical losses of the present methods of agriculture. The farmer's life is now-a-days divided between periods of intolerable labor and demoralizing idleness. Given a national administration of agriculture, and two-thirds of the present force engaged in agriculture would accomplish

55

much more than is now done. In a great country like this the times of stress in the various departments of agriculture so vary that it would probably be possible so to shift the agricultural force from one district to another as to keep it actively engaged in agreeably diversified sorts of culture during the greater part of the year.

Farmer:– Farmers now-a-days have to be home bodies, and don't see much of the world. According to you they would be great travelers. That would be about as big a change in their condition as any you've spoken of.

Smith:– Yes; it would cure one of the greatest drawbacks in the farmer's life in all ages and countries—its lack of variety, its soul-deadening, mind-killing monotony. Speaking of the monotony of the farmer's life today, there is another respect in which nationalism would greatly modify it, and that is its loneliness and lack of social recreations.

Farmer:– Seems as if you were promising about everything.

Smith:– Well, it is true that in proportion as the farmers have in all ages been and today are the most abused set of men on earth as compared with their services to society, the new order of things, by equalizing human conditions, will help them more than any other large class, but I think you'll admit there's nothing extravagant in this particular promise. Under nationalism, in order to induce young men to embrace agriculture, it will have to be made as attractive as other pursuits. It can't be made so if the farmer is to be banished to a log hut five miles from anywhere. The result, under the conditions stated will necessarily be that the farmer will, if he

TO A FARMER

chooses (and his wife will be likely to, anyhow), live in
town like other people and go forth to his work by rail,
if need be. Just as soon as the nation is obliged to make
the conditions of farming agreeable to secure farmers,
they will be made so if it necessitates a railroad to every
farm.

Farmer:– That's great talk. Do you believe it will
ever come to pass?

Smith:– Most assuredly. The western farmers, especially those of Kansas and Nebraska, are largely nationalists already, and all the farmers are bound to be, as
soon as they learn by study and experiment in smaller
and in complete reforms, that nothing save the whole
doctrine of nationalism can right the farmer's wrongs
and break the yoke being prepared for his neck. The
coming national party, whose mission it will be to establish the new nation, will contain pretty liberal contin-
gents from every walk of life, but it will have the farmers as a body pretty nearly from the start.

VIII

Talks on Nationalism—To an Opponent to Paternalism

Mr. Smith, who has joined the nationalist, meets an opponent to paternalism in government.

Opponent to Paternalism:– Join you? I should say not. I am dead against paternalism in government, and always was.

Smith:– What has paternalism got to do with nationalism? We don't propose a paternal government, but on the contrary to establish democracy more perfectly than ever by making the people economically as well as politically equal.

Opponent to Paternalism:– A democratic government may be paternalistic as well as any other.

Smith:– You might as well say that a man can be his own father.

Opponent to Paternalism:– How do you make that out?

Smith:– By the necessary sense of the terms. In a democratic government the people are the government. To say that a democratic government can be a paternal one is to say that the people can stand in a paternal relation to themselves.

TO AN OPPONENT TO PATERNALISM

Opponent to Paternalism:— That is a mere verbal criticism.

Smith:— I beg your pardon, but it is a radical criticism. It rules out of the discussion not merely the term paternalism but the whole line of argument indicated by it, and that is one of the main lines on which nationalism has been attacked. The paternalistic argument against nationalism obviously enough resulted from the attempt of critics to find analogies for nationalism in history; whereas there are no analogies to be found, for the reason that nationalism presupposes a democratic state based upon the equal rights of all. No such state has ever existed till within a century, in this country, and here only partially. In seeking analogies for nationalism, critics have been obliged to draw them from the examples of despotic states in which benevolent monarchs, dealing with their people as children, have undertaken to make them happy, such as, to take a striking example, the system introduced in Peru by the Incas. Between this and all other systems of beneficent despots on the one hand, and the plan of nationalism based upon the absolute political equality of all citizens, operating through the machinery of democratic government, there is the same degree and quality of resemblance that exists between a slave plantation managed by a kind master and a modern business partnership.

Opponent to Paternalism:— That may be so, but the objection to nationalism, as it lies in my mind, you have not yet met. The objection is, that under your system the government is to do everything for the people, and the people nothing for themselves. That is what I op-

59

pose. I hold that the government is best which governs least.

Smith:– I fear you have not yet disentangled yourself from the ruins of the paternalistic argument. Your assumption that the government is something outside of and distinct from the people, applies to a monarchial state, but fails in precise proportion as the state becomes democratic. In a democracy the people are the government, and it is only to a democracy that nationalism is applicable, so that when you say that under nationalism the government is going to do everything for the people, you merely say that the people are going to do everything for themselves, which is quite true. The maxim you quoted is one out of many phrases which were suggested by monarchical conditions, and are simply nonsense as applied to popular governments. It may be true or not in a monarchy that the government is best which governs least; but the saying applied to a popular government simply means that people who do least to regulate and systematize their own business, show most sense, which is not reasonable. You don't call co-operation, paternalism, do you?

Opponent to Paternalism:– Oh no.

Smith:– You do, if you call nationalism paternalism. Government action in a democracy is merely co-operative action. It is the people acting jointly instead of severally. Nationalism simply proposes to extend the scope of their co-operative action to industry. It is nothing but the application of the democratic idea to the business system.

Opponent to Paternalism:– Democracies may be

tyrrannies also. Majorities may oppress minorities and deal with them in a despotic spirit.

Smith:– Undoubtedly that is possible. No form of government is perfect, but we have a democracy already, and I don't understand that the opponents of nationalism want to revert to monarchy. The effect of nationalism will, however, be very much to lessen, as compared with any democratic system hitherto known, the probability of the oppression of one part of the people by another. Where such oppressions have heretofore been practised in democracies they have resulted from the opposing interests and prejudices of different classes of the people or sections of the country. Nationalism, by giving all citizens and sections of the country the same interest in the common weal, not only political but material, will abolish class and sectional interests altogether. All laws will injure or benefit all equally, and a majority anxious to oppress a minority, would have to bite off its nose to spite its face, so to speak.

Opponent to Paternalism:– That is all very fine and perhaps it is all true, but I must confess to being rather a bigoted conservative.

Smith:– I don't think you are. I deny the right of any one to call himself a conservative who opposes nationalism, which is the only adequate proposition yet made for conserving the political rights, moral ideas and material welfare of the people against a stream of tendencies, in politics, society and business, which threatens to undermine them wholly. Who is the conservative: the man who sits still in a tumble-down house till it falls in on him, or he who, seeing the danger, sets to work

61

betimes to put in a new underpinning? You are greatly alarmed over the possibility of a paternal government under nationalism. Let me call your attention to the sort of paternal government which is at present being rapidly established over us.

Opponent to Paternalism:– What is that?

Smith:– Have you not heard of the tendency to the consolidation of the control of the business of the nation in the hands of a few dozen gentlemen, and how rapidly it is proceeding? Have you not heard of the Rockefellers, Goulds, Astors, Vanderbilts, Armours, and the other gentlemen who have elected themselves fathers of the American people, and are taking in hand the children's business?

Opponent to Paternalism:– I should rather say that they were attempting the role of step-fathers.

Smith:– I accept the amendment. It is the power of the father which they are assuming, with the motive of the step-father. But fathers or step-fathers, there is no questioning that we are close upon a time when, unless something intervenes, a few score men, or less, will regulate the affairs and administer the property of the entire people, feeding us, housing us, lighting us, clothing us, carrying us, governing us, working us or starving us, all at their own pleasure and on their own terms. You who are so needlessly afraid of the possibility of paternalism under nationalism, how do you like that kind of step-paternalism with which the country is today confronted?

Opponent to Paternalism:– I don't like it.

Smith:– I presume not. I don't find that the critics

of nationalism like it any better than nationalists do, but they will have to make their choice between it and nationalism soon. Squirm and wriggle as they will, they neither have found nor can find a third alternative to the issue between nationalism and plutocracy. It is the recognition of this fact which is so rapidly making converts to nationalism among the thoughtful men and women of the country. We should be vain indeed if we attributed to our own wit or eloquence the astonishing prevalence of our ideas. It is the economical pressure which is forming our party. It is the plutocrats who are driving the people into our ranks. Do you know why nationalists avoid denouncing their opponents? It is because they know that tomorrow they will be their comrades.

IX

Talks on Nationalism—To a Believer in the Bible

Mr. Smith, who has recently joined the nationalists, meets a friend who opposes nationalism from the stand-point of a believer in the Bible.

Smith:– See here, a man like you ought to be with us. Why are you not?

Believer in the Bible:– I am afraid you will not think much of my reason, for it is not a fashionable one nowadays. The truth is, I am simple-minded enough to believe in the Bible, and my reasons for not joining are based on the inconsistency of your aims with the word of Scripture.

Smith:– Why, that's the last reason I expected to hear any one give for opposing nationalism. We consider the Bible, and especially the New Testament, our best campaign document.

Believer in the Bible:– It is, however, in that very New Testament that I find a declaration which seems to me absolutely fatal to your undertaking. You propose to abolish poverty, but Jesus Christ says, "The poor ye have always with you." Now, I admit your theory is all very plausible, and even admirable, but how is any one going to get over these plain words, if he is, like myself, a believer in the Bible?

TO A BELIEVER IN THE BIBLE

Smith:– Did not Christ also tell his disciples to pray, "Thy kingdom come, Thy will be done on earth as it is in heaven?" Do you believe there is any poverty in heaven?

Believer in the Bible:– Probably not,—of course not.

Smith:– Then you must either believe that Christ taught his disciples to pray for what could never be realized, or else that he contemplated a time when poverty, as well as other evils, would be abolished here on earth. Is there any way of getting over that?

Believer in the Bible:– I confess that the idea in just that form is new to me.

Smith:– It strikes me, then, that you must have been repeating the Lord's Prayer rather inattentively all these years. Somewhere else I believe Christ tells his disciples that two duties sum up all the law and the prophets: one being to love God wholly, the other to love one's neighbor as one's self. Now, how long do you think, if everybody loved his neighbor as himself, there would be left any who were poorer than their neighbors?

Believer in the Bible:– Not long, I presume.

Smith:– Well, what are you going to do about it? Are you going to refuse to obey the command, for fear the supposed prophecy will be damaged? Do you think it will be accepted as a good excuse for disregarding the command, that you were fearful lest it would cause the failure of the prophecy? Don't you think such an excuse would be regarded as rather impertinent?

Believer in the Bible:– But you don't deny that it is a prophecy?

65

TALKS ON NATIONALISM

Smith:— Deny it! Why, of course I deny it. The ascription of a prophetical quality to the expression, "the poor have ye always with you," is, begging your pardon, one of the most ridiculous misinterpretations of a perfectly plain expression which ever obtained currency. Christ was comparing the shortness of his own stay on earth with the relative permanency of poverty. Supposing a man, in comparing two of his clerks, should say that John was uncertain, but that you would always find James at his desk. Would you understand that in his opinion James would be at his post through all eternity? You would understand him as using the word "always" in a relative sense, a sense in which it is used in all languages ten thousand times to one time when it is used for eternity. Seriously, I think you had better go home and get down on your knees, and say your prayers; for if there is any such thing as blasphemy it surely consists in quoting the great apostle of human brotherhood against the abolition of poverty.

Believer in the Bible:— Oh! come, now, that's a hard saying.

Smith:— I beg your pardon. I had no business to say that. But somehow the misquotation of that expression of Christ, to justify the brutalities of society, seems such an outrage to the greatest and tenderest heart which ever beat, that it always makes me angry. If you should see fit to act on the advice I just offered, let me suggest, in connection with your penitential exercises, a course of Scripture readings. There is no better nationalistic literature than the splendid poems in which Isaiah and the other Hebrew seers foretold an era when war and strife should cease, when every man should sit under his own vine and fig-tree, with none to molest or make him afraid, when the lion should lie down with the lamb, and righteousness cover the earth as the waters cover the sea.

Believer in the Bible:- But that is the millennium they are talking about.

Smith:- Well, what of that? Did you suppose that, because it is called the millennium, it was never coming?

Believer in the Bible:- Do you believe that this new era of universal brotherhood and good fellowship, which you nationalists are hoping for, is identical with the millennium predicted in the Scripture?

Smith:- You may call it what you please, I don't care about words. I believe that the world is upon the verge of the realization of the visions of universal peace, love and justice, which the seers and poets of all ages have more or less dimly foreseen and testified of. Of course I do not expect that humanity is to be perfected in a day; but I believe it is about to enter upon an era of progress wholly different from any previous one, not only in the immediate actual improvement and ennobling of human conditions, but still more in the full recognition of the illimitable possibilities of human nature, and the impassioned pursuit of them. No longer, as in previous ages, groping blindly through the night, humanity will be like an army marching swiftly and steadily forward by the light of the day.

Believer in the Bible:- But if this is to be the millennium, Christ must first come again.

Smith:- Well, there is one good sign of his coming,—

the church isn't expecting him. I know nothing about the terms and conditions by which the theologians are fond of hampering divine activity, but if the coming of Christ means his coming in the hearts of men, I advise you to be on the lookout for it. Rent heavens and a descending celestial host would be more spectacular, but it scarcely seems to me, more impressive and more wonderful than the enthusiasm of humanity, the passionate yearning toward brotherhood, which is moving the masses of men today. The clergy discuss wisely how to carry the gospel of Christ to the masses. The gospel is in the masses. I take back what I said about the church not being on the lookout for the second coming. Part of it is. The prophetic parable of the five wise and five foolish virgins is being illustrated in our sight. When the cry arose, "Behold the bridegroom cometh," five had oil in their lamps and went forth to meet him, while the five who had no oil were too late. If I were going to apply that parable to the present situation, I should say that the oil was faith without which the signs of the coming may not be discerned.

Believer in the Bible:– Do you know, Smith, what impresses me most about your talk is its religious tone. I had no idea you were a religious man.

Smith:– All nationalists are religious men. Nationalism is a religion. To fully realize and accept its principle of the brotherhood of men and the responsibility of each to all and all for each, is to be converted, and thenceforth to see all things in a new light.

X

Talks on Nationalism—To a Tariff Reformer

Mr. Smith, who has joined the nationalists, meets a tariff reformer.

Tariff Reformer:– Look here, Smith, perhaps you can tell me something. I've heard a good many nationalist speakers and I've read considerable nationalist literature, but I've been utterly unable, up to date, to find out how nationalists stand on the most important issue of the hour.

Smith:– What is that?

Tariff Reformer:– The tariff issue, of course. Either the nationalists haven't any policy on that question, or else they have unanimously resolved to conceal it.

Smith:– On the contrary, they advocate the most radical policy which is before the public—a policy which, when carried out, will put an end altogether to the tariff question as a political issue.

Tariff Reformer:– I should like to know how they propose to do it.

Smith:– That is easily shown. What is it that makes the tariff a political issue? Is it not the different way in which a tariff affects the welfare of different classes, different business interests and different sections of the

69

country, and the consequent opposition of feeling as to its advantages?

Tariff Reformer:– No doubt that is the ground of the popular interest in the subject, though there is also involved a question of theoretical economics.

Smith:– Certainly; but there is no political issue in a theory which does not appeal to popular interests or popular prejudices as to interests. Our industrial system is made up of classes. It consists of wage-earners, manufacturers, merchants, middlemen, farmers, mine owners and, indefinitely other groups having opposite and irreconcilable interests. Applied to such a variety of opposed interests, any national regulation affecting values, whether of taxation, tariff, finance, or otherwise, necessarily stirs up a very bedlam of contention. Everybody sees, or thinks he sees, how the proposed measure is to give him an advantage over his competitors, or is going to give them an advantage over him, and accordingly favors or opposes it.

Tariff Reformer:– But there is a preponderating common interest, and that represents the right policy.

Smith:– There is no common interest at all. Under the present industrial system, the common interest is a mere abstraction. The only real interests are the particular interests of persons and classes, and these are mutually opposed.

Tariff Reformer:– Be it so; but there is always one of two tariff policies which would help a majority of these opposing interests. That is the course to be followed.

Smith:– It is the course which is followed, undoubted-

TO A TARIFF REFORMER

ly, and with what result? At one election, one set of interests get the majority and destroys the opposed set. At the next election, the defeated interests win more votes and in turn sacrifice their opponents; and so it goes year after year, decade after decade, century in and century out, each one of the periodical changes proving as ruinous to the national wealth in the aggregate as a foreign war.

Tariff Reformer:– Quite right. But you are not consistent. Seeing that you recognize so clearly the ruinous results of the changes in tariff legislation, why not join with us free-traders, and abolish tariffs altogether?

Smith:– Because the abolition of the tariff by free trade would not end the controversy. Quite as many nations have gone back to protection after abandoning it, within the past ten years, as the reverse; in fact, I should say rather more. The so called reformers who seem to think that the adoption of free trade will somehow abolish the tariff issue, are victims of a very silly delusion. There is no more guarantee that free trade, even if established, would survive the first business crisis and subsequent election, than that a prohibitory tariff would. The latter is as much a solution of the tariff problem as the former. There is no final disposition of it, as a disturbing political issue, save that offered by nationalism.

Tariff Reformer:– And what is that?

Smith:– The abolition of opposing business interests in the community. So long as a nation shall be divided into rich and poor, employed and employees, manufacturers and farmers, mine owners, professional classes, tradesmen and middlemen, each having different and materially opposed interests, every change in governmental policy, as to business, will affect them differently, and some will clamor for what others as strenuously oppose. Not only will the feud rage between opposed interests in the same parts of the country, but will become sectional as between different parts of the country, threatening the stability of the nation. Nationalism, by making all citizens, whatever their occupation or wherever resident, equal partners in the aggregate result of their combined industries, will destroy classes and abolish sections.

Tariff Reformer:– But there will still remain the theoretical question whether commodities should ever be produced at a loss at home, rather than imported.

Smith:– When everybody's interest is precisely the same as to the decision of any such question, you may be sure that it will be discussed on its merits, and settled without acrimony. If it be thought desirable to try to introduce a new industry, there is not likely to be any serious objection, because industry not then being in private hands, it will not be necessary to establish an artificial market for the product in question by a tariff, in order to encourage experiments in it. The nation will conduct the experiments at its experimental stations, and, until and unless they succeed, will have no motive to discontinue importing the cheaper foreign product.

Tariff Reformer:– If you bring about the state of things you expect, I will admit that there will be very little left of the tariff as a political issue; but, meanwhile, it is here, and what are you going to do about it?

TO A TARIFF REFORMER

For you cannot deny that it is vitally connected with the prosperity of the country.

Smith:– Certainly I deny it. I do not, of course, question that a tariff may be so framed as to affect the interests of a country more or less favorably, but I do question whether it is at all the potent economical factor for either good or bad which politicians like to make us believe it. Do you suppose the people are fools, not to have seen how easily the protectionists refute the claims of the free-traders on the one hand, and how easily, on the other, the free-traders dispose of the claims of the protectionists? I tell you that the public has at least given attention enough to the arguments of both sides on this tariff question to be convinced that neither tells the truth, and that the tariff issue is mainly a quarrel between the manufacturers and traders, as to which shall have the privilege of fleecing the people. Do you suppose the workingman and the farmer are such fools as not to perceive that the farmer and the artisan are as badly off in free-trade England as in protected America, that on the continent of Europe the misery of the people is the same without the slightest regard to their various tariff systems, and that in Australia, though you step from a free-trade province into a protected one, you would be quite unable to guess it from any difference in the condition of the people? As Lincoln said, "You may fool all the people a part of the time, and a part of the people all the time, but you can't fool all the people all the time." The American people are awaking to the realization that what is the matter with them is not high tariff or low tariff, but the gross economical inequalities of the people and the domination and enslavement of the masses by the money power. It is in vain you try to divert their attention from that question by the tariff issue or any other. They will hold to the fundamental economic issue till it is settled by the advent of nationalism.

XI

Talks on Nationalism—To a Stickler for Private Ownership

Mr. Smith, who has lately joined the na-
tionalists, meets a friend who is a stickler
for private ownership, which he fears na-
ationalism would put an end to.

Stickler for Private Ownership:— There is no need
of talking about the moral excellencies and general at-
tractiveness of your plan. I admit all that. The Lord
knows this is a hard world, as it is, and we take it even
harder than we need. A system under which only a fair
amount of work in a line he chose himself, was expected
of a man; which guaranteed him the same income, sick
or well, young or old, and finally assured him that his
family would be perfectly safe after he died—would be
a very agreeable contrast to the present condition of
things. But human nature is human nature, and man
wants to own things, and you don't propose to let him.
According to nationalism, as I understand it, nobody in
particular is to own anything in particular, but everybody is to own everything in general. Now, I wouldn't
like that. I've a little place of my own, nothing very
fine, but because it is my own I wouldn't swap it for
the lease of a palace. And I notice, too, about my babies, how they always make a big distinction between
what is theirs to use and what is their "ownest own."
Now, my lad, how are you going to fix it up for unrea-

sonable folks like myself and the babies? Mind, I'm not asking for more than my share, but my share I want to be mine.

Smith:– So long as you only want your share, you will find no difficulty under nationalism. The only people who will have any trouble are those who want more than their share. Is it necessary to your happiness to own a railroad?

Stickler for Private Ownership:– Not at all.

Smith:– Do you insist on owning coal-mines, canals, telegraph systems, mills, steamships and such things?

Stickler for Private Ownership:– Not in the least.

Smith:– Well, then, I can assure you that nationalism will not interfere with you at all.

Stickler for Private Ownership:– But I thought under nationalism everything would be owned in common.

Smith:– No doubt you did. If nationalists had been half as active in spreading a correct understanding of nationalism as its opponents have been in disseminating misunderstandings of it, the country would have been converted by this time. The only things the nation will own in common will be the natural resources of the country, and the machinery of industry and commerce. Otherwise people will own, just as they do now, whatever they may care to acquire with their incomes.

Stickler for Private Ownership:– But a man can't own his house, can he?

Smith:– He cannot sell it, nor rent it for profit, nor leave it by will. In those respects his ownership will be limited. In all other respects he will own it a great deal more securely than now, under substantially the same conditions, namely, the payment of dues on it. No man at present can hold a foot of land except on condition of paying taxes to the state, rent to a landlord, or interest on an investment. Let him stop paying taxes and he will soon find his theory that he owns his house exploded. Under nationalism it will be exactly the same way. Every man or woman may pick out the house or lot they choose, if they want to pay the appraised charges on it; and so long as they continue to pay them, they will be absolutely secure in their ownership. The nation guarantees their title. The richest man in America is not so sure of keeping the house he lives in as long as he desires to as every citizen will be under nationalism. You say you own your house, but how much does your ownership amount to when you figure it down to hard facts? Is it free from mortgage?

Stickler for Private Ownership:— No; it isn't. I have a mortgage to pay which is a little larger than I wish it was, but I am in hopes to pay it off in a few years, if business continues good.

Smith:— And yet you speak of owning the house! It seems to me that a man with an imagination strong enough to fancy that he owns a house which he owes a mortgage on, ought to be able to warm his hands over a January sunset. And, by the way, didn't you tell me the other day that your house is in your wife's name?

Stickler for Private Ownership:— Yes. I thought it would be safer, in case I was sued or should fail.

Smith:— Of course. But think what a joke it is for you to talk of "your" house, and the delights of ownership, when upon inquiry it seems that the mortgagee is the first owner, and that what title there is left you have given to your wife as the only way of saving it from your creditors. It strikes me that nationalism would offer you a good deal more substantial sort of ownership than you have now.

Stickler for Private Ownership:– Well, I don't know that I should lose much, that's a fact.

Smith:– Your case is not peculiar. It is typical of the sort of thing people call ownership nowadays, and try to be contented with. Of course, the vast majority of the world do not pretend to own their homes, but merely rent them. The next largest class own them under mortgage, which is, of course, mere sham ownership. Finally, those who own their houses without encumbrance, are liable to be deprived of them any day as a result of a business loss or law-suit. This is not only true of mechanics but of millionaires. There is, in a word, no such thing as ownership in anything now, in the sense of security of possession, and can't be under the present system. We have been speaking of real estate, but the same holds good as to all sorts of personal property. Whatever you have which you do not carry on your person may be your creditor's tomorrow. The very bed you sleep on is liable to be sold from under you, if your business happens to fail. To speak of the haphazard, precarious tenure of property which is alone possible under the present system, as ownership, is a misuse of words. The system of nationalism, so far from destroying the ownership of property, will, by its absolute guarantees to the citizen, for the first time make the ownership of property secure.

XII

Talks on Nationalism—To a Woman's Rights Advocate

Mr. Smith, who has recently joined the nationalists, meets a woman's rights advocate.

Woman's Rights Advocate:– Can you stop a moment Mr. Smith? I want your name on our woman suffrage petition.

Smith:– All right.

Woman's Rights Advocate:– Here is another petition for putting women on the boards of factory inspectors. Will you sign that?

Smith:– Of course.

Woman's Rights Advocate:– I have still something else for you to sign, seeing you are so good-natured. It is a call for a meeting to protest against paying women less than men for the same work. Will you put your name down?

Smith:– Certainly. Have you anything more in the same line?

Woman's Rights Advocate:– Not this morning.

Smith:– Well, then, here's something I want you to sign. Put your name down in that corner.

Woman's Rights Advocate:– Why, this is an application for membership in the Nationalist club. I can't sign that. Why do you expect me to sign that?

Smith:– My general reason is that you are a woman. My particular reason, that you are a woman's rights advocate. A woman who is not in sympathy with nationalism either does not know what her rights are or does not care for them. Unfortunately, one or the other is true of most women as yet. But a woman who advocates the rights of her sex and is not a nationalist is, pardon me, a very inconsistent and slightly absurd person. We are the only real woman's rights party in the world. We alone demand the real equality of women with men.

Woman's Rights Advocate:– How do you make that appear?

Smith:– Simply because the equality of women with men can never be anything but a farce so long as the mass of the feminine sex remains dependent upon the personal favor of men for the means of support.

Woman's Rights Advocate:– Surely, the suffrage could do something for them.

Smith:– I have just signed your petition for that, but not because I regard it as of much importance as an end in itself. I am interested in it merely as an entering wedge for obtaining the economical equality of women with men which nationalism proposes. I tell you frankly that I should be opposed to woman suffrage if I did not look forward to nationalism, because to give the suffrage to a class likely to remain perpetually dependent upon the favor of another class would be to make a mock of it. You might as well give it to a race in a

80

TO A WOMAN'S RIGHTS ADVOCATE

state of partial or complete slavery. It is only when considered as a step towards woman's economical independence that woman suffrage can be intelligently advocated. Until I became a nationalist I confess I saw no sense in it. Why don't you woman suffragists broaden your cause, and make it worth woman's while by going in for economical independence? You will never arouse any enthusiasm among the mass of women till you do.

Woman's Rights Advocate:– We would, if we saw the way to. It is not necessary to say that we should like it very well if we could be pecuniarily independent of our husbands. Much as we may love them, it is not pleasant to go to them for everything. Of course we feel we have a right, but still it comes rather hard.

Smith:– Yes, the married woman's feeling that she has a right no doubt helps her dignity a little, though I fancy it must be hard to tease with dignity, however strong one's sense of right. Really, however, I think the unmarried, grown-up daughter's dependence on her father is far more painful than the wife's upon her husband. The wife feels that she has a right, but the daughter is sensible, perhaps, that she is a burden. To have to beg or wheedle from her father all she needs for herself must be hard for a spirited girl, especially, perhaps, when she sees a younger brother, just out of school, whose cradle possibly she has rocked, with an independent income to spend as he will.

Woman's Right Advocate:– I know all about that. I have sometimes thought that the training in mendicancy which the unmarried daughter goes through, was provi-

81

dentially intended to prepare her for the experiences of a wife. Oh, no, Mr. Smith, you can't tell us women anything we do not already realize as to the humiliation of pecuniary dependence, either as daughters or wives. It is something no amount of love can make tolerable; but is there any way out of it? I confess I see none but to throw open the working-world more and more fully to women, so that they may be self-supporters.

Smith:– That is all very well, but it does not seem to be a remedy for the trouble. In the first place, the wives of course could not generally pursue industry, and even as to the case of the unmarried women, it is no solution. The trouble is, that women are not so strong as men, nor can they, except in a few special lines, do so much work. The average wages of a woman are a mere pittance compared with men's, and even with all unfair discrimination removed they could never equal men's, because they are not nearly so strong. There is the rub. That is the natural, insuperable difficulty in the way of any plan which proposes that women shall depend upon earning their way to equality with men by the market value of their labor. In consenting to make her money-earning power, that is to say her industrial productiveness, the measure of her economical claims, woman makes a fatal mistake.

Woman's Rights Advocate:– But what measure shall she set up for her rights, if not that?

Smith:– Her claim upon the race as burden bearer for it. Why is she weaker than man, and less capable as a worker? Is it not because she bears a cross for humanity, while he walks freely? Her weakness is a

TO A WOMAN'S RIGHTS ADVOCATE

title, more sacred than his strength, to all the fruits of the human heritage.

Woman's Rights Advocate:– Yes, I know it. We all know that; but these are only fine words. We have always had plenty of fine words. It is of no use to talk about a claim that is a mere general one on society at large. We cannot sue society for our rights, however plain they are.

Smith:– It is precisely to remedy this difficulty that nationalism has come.

Woman's Rights Advocate:– How do you propose to remedy it?

Smith:– By an organization of society which shall enable it to discharge its collective debts and enforce its collective rights. The human inheritance comes down to us as the result of innumerable ages of labor, struggle, achievement and martyrdom on the part of a common and blended ancestry. It is absolutely an estate in common. Hitherto this most obvious fact has been utterly disregarded. There has been no attempt at an organization to administer the estate in the common interest, but the strong heirs have seized what they could get and keep, the weak heirs being downtrodden. This ancient, immeasurable, wrong, nationalism proposes to remedy, by making the nation assume the trusteeship of the common estate for the common and equal benefit of all the heirs, whether men or women, strong or weak. If they have inherited weakness, that measures their claim upon the estate; if they have inherited strength, that is their debt to the estate. If their weakness be owing to womanhood, it is a twice sacred title.

TALKS ON NATIONALISM

Woman's Rights Advocate:– The nation is going to be very good to us.

Smith:– Good to you? No; only at last just. The denial to women of an equal and independent share in the world has been, up to this time, the greatest crime of humanity. But nobody was to blame for it, in particular, and it could never be remedied to all eternity so long as particular women could only appeal for their rights to particular men, however generous the latter might be. Their claim, like that of all the weaker heirs, was upon the estate and against society collectively, and could never be met until society should be collectively organized. And that leads me back to the point I started from, which was, I believe, that woman's rights advocates who are not nationalists do not know what they are talking about.

Woman's Rights Advocate:– I don't know but I shall end by agreeing with you. Tell me more about the details of woman's position under your plan.

Smith:– Like every other citizen, after attaining the years of citizenship, she will be required, if physically or mentally able, to do such sort of work, physical or intellectual, as she shall (subject to proof of fitness) elect to do. This requirement will, of course, not be allowed to interfere with marriage and its consequences. Her means of support will be an income equal to that of all citizens, and whether she be married or unmarried, will be her personal right, and received through no other person. She will, that is to say, through life, be not only economically equal with every man, but absolutely inde-

84

TO A WOMAN'S RIGHTS ADVOCATE

pendent of any man. Her account for duty and maintenance will be with the nation.

Woman's Rights Advocate:— After all, that would be only fair and just, though it seems so much. Mr. Smith, I think you are right. All the women are bound to be nationalists when they find out what you mean.

Smith:— I am perfectly sure of that. Ours is the cause of the oppressed and of those who have no helper, everywhere, whether men or women, but it is particularly and emphatically the cause of women. The program of nationalism is woman's Declaration of Independence.

XIII

Talks on Nationalism—To a Working-man

Mr. Smith, who has joined the nationalists, meets a workingman.

Workingman:– No, sir; not any for me. Poor men who work for a living can't afford to waste their time on theories. Fine words butter no parsnips. I dare say it would be very fine if we could have things fixed up for us as you fellows propose, but we might as well cry for the moon. Propose something practical,—something that will help them right off,—and workingmen will listen to you.

Smith:– Would you like to make sure of keeping your job? Would you call that something practical?

Workingman:– Very practical.

Smith:– Well, that is what nationalism means. It is a plan for helping men to keep their jobs.

Workingman:– It will meet a long-felt want, if it will do that.

Smith:– Well, it will, for that's just what nationalism, boiled down, amounts to. It's a way for helping every man to keep his job.

Workingman:– How is it going to help him?

Smith:– Let us be practical, as you say, and stick to facts. You are a railroad man, aren't you?

Workingman:– Yes.

TO A WORKINGMAN

Smith:- You want to know how nationalism is going to help you keep your job on the road?

Workingman:- That's about the size of it. Tell me that, and I'll join. Mary and the kids would like to know, too.

Smith:- One of the first things we want to do is to nationalize the railroads.

Workingman:- You mean to have government take them.

Smith:- Yes, take them and run them.

Workingham:- Well, I don't know how that is going to help me. It would only be changing bosses.

Smith:- It would be getting done with boss rule altogether, and becoming, instead, a member of a service in which the rights of every person, from bottom to top, were guaranteed by law.

Workingman:- Now you are beginning to talk! Let's hear some more about that.

Smith:- What nationalism proposes is this: That when the government takes the railroads the present force of men be taken into the public service just as it stands, every man keeping his place. No man would after that be liable to discharge, except for cause, after a fair hearing. Promotions would no more be by favor, over the heads of equally deserving men, but would be by merit, as shown by record. Every man's pay would go on in case of sickness or accident, and when he became too old to work he would be pensioned.

Workingman:- There'd be a rush for jobs of that sort, I guess.

Smith:- No doubt there would be a big rush; but

when people saw the advantages of the system, they would not be long in nationalizing other sorts of business, until at last not merely railroad employees but everybody was sure of his job.

Workingman:– What I'm thinking is, that there would be such a rush for those government jobs at first that a fellow would need a big "pull" to get one.

Smith:– On the contrary, if the nationalist plan is carried out, no amount of "pull" would help a man to get a job. You saw Gen. Tracy's plan for keeping politics out of the navy-yards. Well, that is as mild as milk compared with the nationalist idea of a proper civil service admission test. In the first place, all further admission, to a nationalized body of workers, after it had been taken over, would be to the lowest grade. Everybody after that would have to work up from the ranks. In order to be a candidate, a person would have to possess certain fixed qualifications.

Workingman:– I hope you would not expect a fellow who wanted to be fireman to pass an examination in Latin.

Smith:– Of course not. The qualifications he would have to show would be those necessary for the position he was trying for, and no others. The candidates having the biggest percentage of qualifications would get the jobs. There would not be any discretion allowed in appointing them, and they would be indebted to nobody but themselves for their places. Of course after men were once admitted, promotions would be only by record, and the incompetent man would either be dismissed or would remain in the lowest grades.

TO A WORKINGMAN

Workingman:– But if you dismiss a man from national employment when there are no private employers left, you'll starve him.

Smith:– I was only speaking of the beginnings of nationalism. Afterward, of course, when there is no private employment, there will be no dismissing. A fellow then who cannot do one sort of work will be found another sort. Even the insane and invalids will be found something to do.

Workingman:– What if there should be a strike on one of your nationalized businesses? What would you do then?

Smith:– I don't see why the effect should be any worse than that of a strike now, while the likelihood of a strike would be reduced to almost nothing by the advantages the new system would offer to the men. It would be a strong provocation which would induce men to forfeit a life position, with a pension to boot; don't you think so?

Workingman:– Well, it would, that is a fact.

Smith:– For that matter, if the provocation were great enough, I should hope they would strike, and succeed, too.

Workingmen:– I see a good deal in the papers about what the nationalists are trying to do to get the power for cities to own their own gas-works. I suppose you would have that force organized in the same manner?

Smith:– Certainly, if we can have our way. It is common to discuss this municipal lighting business as if the consumers' benefit were the chief gain by it. But the subject has a side quite as interesting to the employees in those businesses, and the same is true of the question of city ownership of the street railroads. The street-car men are all bound to be nationalists, as soon as they understand what we are driving at.

Workingman:– How soon do you believe all this can be brought about? I should like to enjoy a little of it myself.

Smith:– It will be brought about just as soon as the intelligent workingmen of the country find out what nationalists are trying to do for them, and come to our support with their votes. They are beginning to find out already. Nationalism can no longer be twitted as a "kid-glove" movement. The workingmen are swelling its ranks very rapidly. A good many of them at first shared your notion that it was nothing but a fine-spun theory, but as they come to examine it they are bound to discover that it is the only really practical labor party in the world. It is as I told you, when you boil it down, a plan to help men to find jobs and then to keep them. Let that idea once get into the heads of the people, and the present industrial system will not last much longer.

Workingman:– Count me in. I don't know about joining your club, for you see I have a night run and could not be at the meetings, but maybe I can help a little by spreading the news among the boys. There are a good many of them that haven't fairly got on to it, any more than I had; and look here, you can count in Mary and the kids, too. Mary is dead against my having anything to do with strikes, but when she hears there's a party that's going to help me keep my job, she'll work for it, you bet, and she's a hustler.

XIV

Talks on Nationalism—To a Father of a Family

Mr. Smith, who has joined the nationalists, meets a friend who is the father of a family.

Smith:— Why, bless my soul, man, here you are actually standing still! What's the matter?

Father of Family:— Missed my horse-car.

Smith:— Ah, that explains it. This is the first time I have seen you, except on a run, for a year.

Father of Family:— I am pretty busy, that's a fact.

Smith:— Why do you work yourself to death? If you are bound to commit suicide why not take some easier way?

Father of Family:— I've got a family to provide for.

Smith:— Well, you certainly don't have any difficulty in earning enough for their keep.

Father of Family:— It isn't that. I can take care of them so long as I am around, if I keep my health, but I may drop out you know, and I want to provide for them in that event, which makes it necessary that I should lay up a little property; do you see?

Smith:— The worst of it is, as things go nowadays, even when a man succeeds in leaving his family a little something he can feel no assurance that it will not be stolen by trustees or lost by a bad investment before he has been dead five years. I suppose you heard of the case of Jack Harding's widow, didn't you? They say she is applying to her old friends for sewing to do, and is glad to take gifts of clothing for her children, the babies Jack was so proud of. I understand her friends are trying to induce her to give them away, for she is actually unable to provide for them properly. I hope Jack doesn't know about it. Poor fellow, one of the last things he said to me was that he didn't mind dying as he would if he were not leaving his family well fixed.

Father of Family:– Yes, it's a pretty tough case, and I suppose it might as well be your wife's or mine as Jack's. In times like these, when it is more than a clever business man can always do to detect frauds and find safe investments, how is a woman going to do it? All we can do is to leave behind all we can and hope for the best.

Smith:– I can't agree with you there. That isn't the best we can do. I want to talk to you a minute about a new system of life insurance, which I have lately become interested in, and which seems to be better than anything I had heard of before.

Father of Family:– Look here, Smith, you don't mean that you are a life insurance agent in disguise! If you've been working this confidence business just to—

Smith:– Don't be alarmed. I'm not a life insurance agent in the usual sense, and represent no company that exists. It's on an altogether new plan, and a big thing. I should like to have you come in on the ground floor.

TO A FATHER OF A FAMILY

Father of Family:— Is it a mutual insurance concern?

Smith:— Strictly mutual.

Father of Family:— How many people are in with you?

Smith:— Well, I think there may be half a million who are about ready for it.

Father of Family:— Half a million! Well, I should say that would be enough to start with. How many more do you want?

Smith:— We want the rest of the nation.

Father of Family:— That's modest. What do you call this mammoth system?

Smith:— Nationalism.

Father of Family:— Oh, I see. I remember hearing that you were in with those fellows. I have seen more or less about nationalism in the papers, but I hadn't noticed that it was a life insurance company.

Smith:— That's just what it is. It proposes to write for every member, men and women alike, an endowment policy. The peculiarity of the policy is that it becomes due at the birth of the policy-holder and continues to be payable during life as a yearly income sufficient for maintenance. As every man's wife and children have these policies as well as himself, he is relieved from anxiety for their welfare after his own death, knowing that they will always be safe from want or humiliation.

Father of Family:— A pretty big scheme, I should say.

Smith:— It has to be big to meet the need.

Father of Family:— For such a comprehensive insurance as you propose to have the nation undertake, a pretty heavy premium would have to be charged.

93

Smith:– The premium will average no larger than everybody is now paying for the very poor sort of insurance derived from the possession of a little money which may be swept away to-morrow, namely, his labor during manhood in his chosen occupation. For that matter, it is believed that the co-operative methods of industry proposed in connection with this insurance system will make the amount of labor necessary to secure the new insurance far less than is now required to keep up the smallest-sized bank account.

Father of Family:– But if I understand the plan of the nationalists, the earnings of everybody are to be pooled as the fund from which everybody is to be guaranteed maintenance.

Smith:– Precisely.

Father of Family:– But supposing I can earn more than another man. Don't I lose by pooling results with him?

Smith:– You do not lose so much in amount as you gain in security. Let us suppose that the money you acquired to support your old age and to leave to your wife and children would be greater if you had kept it in a separate pile; on the other hand, it would in that case be liable to total loss by any accident, leaving you to die in the poor-house; and if your family inherited it, they likewise would hold it in the same insecure way. Surely one would prefer to leave his family a secure income of $1,000 rather than a precarious one of thrice that.

Father of Family:– That is true, of course, I admit that the rule, the greater the security the less the income, is a fair one. But the other fellow, who could not under the present system leave his family half what I can, would profit a great deal more than I would by the equality plan. As between him and me, it would be unfair.

Smith:– I hope you would not be prevented from a course which would unquestionably benefit you because it would benefit another man more still.

Father of Family:– I should not be so bad as that, but it seems as if your plan were lacking in not providing some way for securing the better man the larger claim.

Smith:– That would be impossible, consistently with the ground principle of this sort of insurance, which is the moral and economic solidarity of society, and its responsibility toward all its members, not merely of the present generation, but of past and future ones. Don't be so sure, by this way, because you are cleverer than your neighbor, that you are cheated by pooling your product with his. His children or grandchildren may be cleverer than yours, and thus redress the balance. In a large business like this which we propose, carried on from generation to generation, such balances are very likely to redress themselves ultimately. Whatever a hopeless old bachelor might say against the equality of insurance, I am sure that no father of children will, on reflection, object to it. Let us suppose that you have been pretty successful in life, have earned more than other men, and so far have gained by the present system of economic inequality; are you sure that your children will be as strong and keen as you are? If not, they in turn will be losers by the principle of inequality you contend for. For the sake of riding on other men's backs while you live, are you willing to take the chances of their riding on the backs of your children after you are dead?

Father of Family:– No, no. You are right.

Smith:– It seems to me that any father or mother in the land, who can be induced to consider this principle of economical equality with reference to the future of their children, must agree that it is the strongest of all arguments for the insurance system that nationalism proposes. There is no device given under heaven, by which you can guard your wife from suffering and indignity, save by a system which shall guard all men's wives. There is no way by which you can be sure of protecting your children from wrong and want save by a system which shall protect all men's children. So long as the pit of poverty is permitted to yawn by the way of life, it is as likely to be your wife, or child, or grandchild, as another's, who falls into it. It must be filled up, and the men or women who refuse to help in the work invite responsibility for the blood of their own offspring. There is no security in selfishness.

XV

Talks on Nationalism—To a Pessimist

Mr. Smith, who has joined the nationalists, meets a pessimist, who maintains that human nature must be changed before nationalism will be possible.

Pessimist:– Make human nature over again, and your scheme might work.

Smith:– Human nature needs improvement, no doubt, and nationalism will establish conditions more favorable to its improvement than any which has existed heretofore. Meanwhile, however, it is in quite good enough condition already for nationalism to make a start.

Pessimist:– Smith, your hopefulness is sometimes so extravagant that it has a positively depressing effect on a reasonable man. Take a look around on the world as it is, and tell me seriously, if you can be serious, how much brotherly kindness, generosity, self-devotion and unselfishness you see in the actual relation of people.

Smith:– A very great deal—a wonderful deal.

Pessimist:– Well, I wish I had your eyes.

Smith:– Your eyes are well enough, but you don't look in the right spots.

Pessimist:– Spots! Oh yes, there are spots, no doubt, where the virtues you want can be found existing,

97

but I didn't understand that you proposed to limit your system to spots, but to apply it generally.

Smith:– So we do; it is from the existence already of the desired virtues in spots that we base our confidence upon the possibility of their general cultivation.

Pessimist:– I don't see how; I should rather say that the limitations of the virtues in question to these few spots, after a long period of human development, was calculated to discourage any idea that they could be generally cultivated.

Smith:– That might be a natural first impression, but it is not a scientific deduction. Supposing, upon close study of the conditions under which mutual confidence and affection now exist, we devise a plan for making those conditions general: is it not scientific, then, to believe that their growth can be proportionally extended?

Pessimist:– No doubt, provided you can be sure what the true conditions of their growth are, and can really make them general.

Smith:– I think I can satisfy you about that. Let us see what are the conditions under which relations of mutual affection and trust at present exist. The average man, nowadays, lives a sort of double life—a Jekyll-Hyde existence. In his work-a-day life he is a sort of Hyde; not, of course, of necessity a very wicked person, but hard, suspicious, keen, stern, cunning, overbearing, underreaching. That is the way he has to make his living. In this character, he is essentially not lovable, and it is no wonder that people don't love him. If they trusted him they would lose by him. But follow this fellow as he goes home at night. Now he is Jekyll. You will find that his children adore him, his wife loves him, his brothers trust him, and he has a band of friends and associates every one of whom has implicit faith in him. Within this little circle of relatives and friends there reigns a mutual confidence, a trustfulness, a generosity, which far exceed any reasonable estimate of the grade of social sentiment needed to enable nationalism to begin business.

Pessimist:– But these are either kin of blood, or else selected friends. The circle is so mutually trustful only because it is limited.

Smith:– No doubt each particular circle is limited; but everybody has such a circle, and most people belong more or less intimately to several such circles. Now, it is common for us to assume, no doubt half-unconsciously, that our particular circle of friends consists of persons of quite peculiar merits; but this is not scientific. It is, indeed, nothing but rank egotism. Reason will compel us to admit that probably our luck has only been about the average luck as to friends, as in other respects. The result is rather startling; it amounts to admitting that other people and their friends are about as good as we and our friends. When a person has sincerely admitted this he is about ready to be a nationalist, for probably most people feel that if the nationalistic experiment were confined to them and their circle it might succeed, owing to the excellent and unusual qualities of themselves and their friends.

Pessimist:– I admit your point to some extent. It is true, as you say, that all or nearly all people trust and are trusted by some group of friends and associates. I admit that pretty nearly everybody is in this way shown to be, under proper conditions, capable and deserving of the social sympathy which nationalism calls for. But I don't see how that helps your case. How are you going to bring these groups together? Why do groups of friends and acquaintances now trust each other? Because special circumstances or long acquaintance has taught them they can do so safely. How are you going to give them the same confidence toward strangers and the mass of men?

Smith:– Ah! There is just where nationalism comes in. Why is it that men so naturally distrust each other that long acquaintances or peculiar circumstances only can breed confidence in one another's intentions? It is owing to the fact that, under the present system of business, we have to make our living out of one another, preying upon our fellows and being preyed on by them. How to make something out of the other man, and how to prevent the other from making anything out of him, is the first thought of any two persons brought together in business, and too often in so-called social relations. It is this blended impulse of rapacity and apprehensions, suggested and even necessitated by our social system, which makes sympathy and trust so difficult and even so unnatural in our relations with men in general. But only let us become convinced that another person has no idea of profiting by us, and how quickly do we put trust in him to any extent! Who has not noticed how soon a feeling of comradeship and mutual devotion is engendered between men, strangers before, by circumstances which, by establishing some sort of partial community of interests between them, give them an excuse to lay

100

aside their natural suspicion. There is no stronger attribute of human nature than this hunger for comradeship and mutual trust. Nationalism will satisfy it by putting an end, utterly and absolutely, alike to the fear that others may live on us, and the hope that we may succeed in living on them.

Pessimist:– And then, I suppose, everybody will be everybody's else bosom friend.

Smith:– I don't expect so. Intimacy depends upon natural affinities, and very possibly one's circle of intimates may be no larger than now; but it is certainly reasonable to believe that a general sense of comradeship, mutual good feeling, and enthusiasm in co-operation for the common good, will be the natural consequence of a system based on the guarantee that no one can use any one else for his own profit, and that no one can gain anything except through and by the common good.

XVI

Talks on Nationalism—To a Charitable Worker

Mr. Smith, who has recently joined the nationalists, meets a charitable worker connected with the church, who objects to nationalism on the ground that it will leave no occasion for charity.

Smith:– Why is it that you are not one of us? You are so much interested in benevolent undertakings that one would suppose you just the woman to be taken with a plan to do away with poverty altogether. I suppose you are afraid the plan would not work.

Charitable Worker:– I don't know whether it would work or not, but I am afraid it would be a bad thing, if it did work.

Smith:– The abolition of poverty a bad thing! Surely you can't mean that!

Charitable Worker:– Not in itself, but in its moral effect in the long run upon human nature, for the reason that the equality of human conditions would leave no further play for the graces of pity, generosity and gratitude—in short, for charity.

Smith:– But, bless your heart, those graces were called forth to ameliorate human suffering. Would you make them the excuse for perpetuating that suffering? Would you hold on to the disease for the sake of the medicine? Would you keep a pond open in the garden for the children to fall into, so that they might cultivate heroism by saving one another from drowning? For the matter of that, you quite mistake in assuming that, because everybody would have food and clothes enough, there would be no occasion for pity, sympathy and generosity. Have you never any occasion for those feelings toward your well-to-do friends and relatives?

Charitable Worker:— Oh, yes.

Smith:— You'll excuse me for saying that it seems a shockingly narrow definition of charity to confine it to almsgiving. St. Paul gives the most exhaustive and generally accepted definition of charity on record, in I Corinthians, chap. xiii, and the only reference he makes to almsgiving or material benefactions is to expressly state that they are not to be confounded with charity at all.

Charitable Worker:— Yes, I remember that passage.

Smith:— So it appears that poverty is not needed to call forth charity—as Paul understands it,—but that occasions for it must continue to arise as long as human nature remains imperfect.

Charitable Worker:— But so much of religion has always consisted in giving. I mean in almsgiving.

Smith:— No doubt it has. No doubt a great many people in past ages have derived a profitable spiritual reaction from gifts to the poor, but the time is past, or fast passing, when anybody, but a narrow-minded person can give with any sense of virtue.

103

Charitable Worker:– Why, what do you mean?

Smith:– I refer to the profound change which the new economics, combined no doubt with important moral tendencies, have made in the ideas of people as to the rights of property as at present distributed. The title of a man to his possessions, however honestly acquired, is no longer regarded by himself or by the world as anything at all like the absolute thing it was regarded a generation ago. The rich man who gives away a million or so to public purposes, now-a-days, is no longer looked upon as a person who places the world in his debt, but rather as one who has attempted to make some slight indirect restitution of what he owed the world. Of course, there are plenty of rich brutes; but the better sort of rich men are getting shamefaced about their money. The growing recognition of the injustice of the present economical system has placed them on the defensive. If they are men of heart and conscience, they feel as if their wealth made them accomplices with that system, because, even though innocently, they have profited by its injustice.

Charitable Worker:– That reminds me of what one of the richest girls I know was saying the other day. She declared she wished she had been born a hundred years ago, for it was no fun to be rich now unless one had a heart like a stone. She is really a very tender-hearted girl, and I actually think her money makes her miserable. She told me that when a beggar thanked her for a dime, she felt like saying, "Forgive me for having anything to give you."

Smith:– She has got at the heart of the matter, and

represents the feeling of a great and increasing number. When all the good folks see the matter as she does, and they are fast growing to do so, nationalism will come quickly as the only solution of an intolerable situation. As for charity in the sense of a moral relation between rich and poor, the new economics are already making it obsolete without waiting for nationalism. The rich have no moral satisfaction in giving what they half feel is not their own, while the poor man resents receiving as a gift what he feels is somehow his right. Of course, this period of transition to the new era of equality and its new moralities is disagreeable, but the result surely will be wholly good. The relations of rich and poor, far from having been morally edifying to the race, have been the most demoralizing influence it has suffered from. The spectacle of suffering which is recognized to be inevitable and remediless hardens the heart. Where it moves a few to commiseration and self-sacrifice, it educates the many to a habit of indifference. Sympathy is aroused by like circumstances, and repelled by unlike. The poor are strangers to the well-to-do, and almsgiving is mostly a cold, perfunctory thing. It is in our relations with our own class that moral emotions are chiefly called out, and therefore the equalizing of human conditions will mean the broadening of human sympathy.

Charitable Worker:– I do not feel sure that you may not be right. Indeed, you must not think that I objected to nationalism on the ground I did, from any serious conviction of my own. I am ashamed to say that I have not thought much about it—not so much as I shall. In saying that poverty was a God-ordained condition, I was, I imagine, just echoing some things our rector said in a sermon last Sunday.

Smith:– Yes, yes, I know. Some men who, I am bound to believe and do believe, are good men, have said this, and are saying it. I presume they are very sure that their children will never fall into the pit which they insist on keeping open. I suppose the church has for so long regarded the poor as its charge, that it feels a little as a faithful nurse does, who, having been long wonted to care for a patient, and become devoted to her task, is told that he is about to make a cure and will need her services in that line no more. Of course, when the nurse has time to think it over, she will see how absurd her attitude is, and so will the church.

XVII

Talks on Nationalism—To a Skeptical Friend

Mr. Smith, who has recently joined the nationalists, discourses with a skeptical friend upon the meaning of the "Brotherhood of Men."

Skeptical Friend:— See here, Smith, I have been wanting to pick a bone with you for some time. I see in the public discussions of you fellows who call yourselves nationalists, a great deal about the brotherhood of men.

Smith:— Yes; that is the moral basis of nationalism.

Skeptical Friend:— Then you do mean something by it. I did not know but it was a mere bit of rhetoric used to catch the sentimentalist voter, so to speak.

Smith:— I can assure you there is no feature of our faith that we are more in dead earnest about, or more anxious to impress upon people's minds.

Skeptical Friend:— Well, then, since you do really mean something by it, perhaps you will have the goodness to explain to me what it is you mean, for I confess the phrase seems to me obvious nonsense. It appears to me too plain to need statement that no man is my brother unless he be the son of my father and mother.

Smith:– In the natural sense of course he is not. In the moral sense he is. What we mean is that all men are brothers in the sense of owing one another the same duties and obligations that children of the same two parents do, and that society should be reorganized in accordance with that principle.

Skeptical Friend:– Of course the conclusion follows if the premise is granted, but I dispute the premise. It is a pure piece of assumption, which only a sentimentalist would let pass unchallenged.

Smith:– Do you believe that natural brothers, children, I mean, of the same pair of parents, have any duties toward each other?

Skeptical Friend:– Of course.

Smith:– What is the ground of those duties?

Skeptical Friend:– Why, natural affection, I suppose.

Smith:– Some brothers are not fond of each other. Does this lack of natural affection discharge them from duties to each other.

Skeptical Friend:– I suppose not. I never particularly thought of the matter, but I presume that their common parentage is the ground of their duties to each other as brothers.

Smith:– Very evidently, for it is only by virtue of that common parentage that their relations differ from those of other people. Any peculiar duties they have toward each other must therefore be based on this fact. Let us see just what the basis is. Parents having directly caused the existence of their children, owe them the utmost devotion and protection which it is in their power to give. On the other side, children are indebted

TO A SKEPTICAL FRIEND

to their parents for their lives and all which life brings them, and thus owe a filial obligation. Is it not so?

Skeptical Friend:– Of course. You have stated mere truisms. I don't see what they have to do with the natural duties of brothers.

Smith:– That is what we come to now. If I have assets in my hands on which you have a claim, and you are indebted to a third party, I must account for them to the third party. A son owes all he is and has to his parents, who in turn have an indefinite responsibility of protection and devotion to his brother, their other son. Therefore, the one son owes to the other the indefinite service of all his powers. If he fails to render it, he repudiates his debt to his parents, and deprives himself of any moral title to his own life.

Skeptical Friend:– By George, you make out a strong case. Do you know you almost make me glad I have no brothers? It might be too burdensome.

Smith:– I am going to show you that you have a great many brothers.

Skeptical Friend:– You mean everybody. Well, I don't see that you have made much headway in doing that. I don't see what the argument for the duties of a man to his natural brother has to do with his brotherly duty to all men.

Smith:– It has everything to do with it. The one argument involves the other. The man who denies that all men owe one another the duties of brothers denies the duties of natural brothers.

Skeptical Friend:– I must be very dull, for I confess I don't see it.

TALKS ON NATIONALISM

Smith:– The immediate parents of any man are but the last pair of an indefinite, untraceable ancestry, which at no remote period becomes inextricably blended with that of the entire community, or nation, and eventually with the race itself. Every one has, not only two, but millions of parents. He is, in fine, the offspring of mankind, and his mother is humanity. This complex parentage, identical with mankind, is that which has formed him and determined him from the very rudiments of human nature. His immediate parents have done little more than to transmit to him, with a few superficial impressions from themselves, the moral, physical and intellectual inheritance of the race. It is evident that if the immediate parents are so heavily responsible to their child for the bare fact of his existence the responsibility of the race for him is infinitely greater, seeing that he is so incomparably much more a product of the race than of any two parents. Correspondingly greater and more absolute is his debt for all he is and has to the race, that is, the sum of past generations, than to his immediate parents. To the precise extent to which he is indebted to the race, he is charged with the responsibilities of the race for its other offspring, who are his fellow-men. That is to say, he owes them the duty natural brothers owe each other on precisely similar but far stronger grounds. If the natural brother who denies his fraternal duty repudiates his debt to his parents and has no title to life, so does he who refuses to see a brother in every fellow-man, and so to treat him. He has no business on the earth. He has embezzled himself.

Skeptical Friend:– Well, I'll admit that you have

made out a better argument for the brotherhood of men than I thought you could. I had no idea there was so much to be said for it, or, indeed, anything. It's a belief that brings a pretty heavy responsibility with it. I should not want to accept it until I was very sure of it.

Smith:– I beg you won't. There are people enough already who talk about human brotherhood without meaning it. I don't advise you to believe this doctrine of the brotherhood, anyhow, if you think much of your own comfort.

Skeptical Friend:– Why not?

Smith:– Because the present order of society is based on the absolute repudiation of any such brotherhood whatever; and because, from the moment you come to believe in the brotherhood, this state of things will seem so intolerable to you that you will be able to do nothing else by night or day but strive and plan for an utter change, and the work is very great.

XVIII

Talks on Nationalism—To Jones

Mr. Smith, who has joined the nationalists, meets Jones, who ridicules nationalism as a plan for pensioning everybody.

Jones:– Did you see Prof. ———'s lecture in the paper this morning? He got off a good thing on you fellows; said that nationalism was just a plan for pensioning everybody. Seems to me that he hit you off pretty well.

Smith:– You think any plan of that sort ridiculous on the face of it, do you?

Jones:– I must say I do.

Smith:– You feel quite sure about it, do you?

Jones:– There's no doubt about it, not the least.

Smith:– Well, that shuts out the Germans, the French, the Swiss and the English.

Jones:– What do you mean?

Smith:– I mean that Germany, Switzerland and France either have already adopted the plan of pensioning the people on a large scale, or are about to do so, and that the British Parliament at the next session will undoubtedly consider and may probably pass a similar law, of which Joseph Chamberlain, the liberal leader, will

112

be sponsor, with strong support, both liberal and conservative.

Jones:– I am astonished to hear that.

Smith:– If you read the papers you would not be. The fact is the idea that nationalism can be made to appear ridiculous by calling it a general pensioning plan, exceeds the average attack on it in the crass ignorance it displays of contemporary facts and tendencies, economic and governmental. In so far as it is true it only indicates that nationalism is in line with one of the leading movements of the day.

Jones:– What are these laws like for pensioning people? Are they for everybody?

Smith:– Not yet. They are for workingmen and are intended to provide for their maintenance in sickness and age.

Jones:– And the pensions are paid out of taxes?

Smith:– Not wholly. A good part is, but the rest is made up out of contributions from the working-man himself and from his employer. According to the pending French law, after reaching 65 the working-man who comes under this law will receive a regular annual pension, supposed to be enough for an economical support without another stroke of work on his part.

Jones:– Well, no man ought to have to work after 65, that is a fact. If he has been half industrious he has earned in that time a right to rest.

Smith:– But as a matter of fact millions do work on beyond that age, and indeed until they fall into the grave. Our infernal industrial system spares age as little as it does infancy. It grinds up grandfather and grandchild together.

Jones:– It is pretty bad, I admit. The world is a hard one, but still I can't see that it quite follows because a man is in a bad fix that it is the government's business to help him out.

Smith:– Government is bound to secure a man bare justice at least, isn't it? It is bound to secure him what he has earned.

Jones:– Certainly.

Smith:– Well, did not you yourself just say that a man ought not to have to work after 65, because he had fairly earned a right to rest after that?

Jones:– Certainly, he has earned it in justice, but not in law.

Smith:– That's a good reason why a new law should be made. Justice is not based on the law; it is the law that should be based on justice. Since the law fails to secure the worker rest in age which by common agreement he has fairly earned, it represents a failure of justice which the state is bound to rectify. Not one in ten thousand of the claims which get laws made to secure them and courts to enforce them, have behind them half this obvious and substantial justice which supports the title of the life-long toiler to rest and security in old age, which the nations are at last beginning to recognize and vindicate. I tell you, my friend, the time is at hand when society is going to be reconstructed upon the basis of half a dozen just such broad, substantial principles of obvious justice as that.

Jones:– That may all be, but as to this particular

114

proposition, the question arises, who is going to pay the pensions when everybody is pensioned? When everybody has a pension won't it amount to the pensioners paying their own pensions?

Smith:– Of course it will.

Jones:– Seems to me it is a pretty bad give-away, Smith. Excuse me if I smile. I did not suppose you would be trapped into admitting that!

Smith:– Admit it? Why, I assert it. You are insured, aren't you?

Jones:– Yes, I carry $5,000.

Smith:– Very good; when the insurance is paid upon maturity of the policy, will it be a favor this company does or what you have earned?

Jones:– It will be what I have earned, of course.

Smith:– Precisely. It is you after all then who pay your own policy. The insurance system is merely a device for helping you to provide for the future out of the present. That is all which any system of universal pensioning or guaranteeing of maintenance to its members by the nation would be. There is nothing more fanciful in the principle about such a scheme, however extensive, than about any form of insurance, except that the bigger the scale of insurance the safer it is.

Jones:– And do you think it would be practicable to introduce such a scheme as this French or German one here in America?

Smith:– Not without modifications. In quoting these European schemes I did not mean to indorse them in details but only to show the tremendous progress which this nationalistic idea of a general guarantee of maintenance

115

to the people, which our American critics find so foolish, is actually making among the most conservative nations. As hitherto adopted or as likely to be adopted in Europe or England, the idea is, however, only a half-way nationalism, and therefore logically incomplete.

Jones:— How is that?

Smith:— According to nationalism a nation is not in a position safely to guarantee the maintenance of its members until and in so far only as it provides and directs their employment. Thus only can it make sure of having, out of the product of their labor, the wherewithal to make good the guarantee without running behind. To pledge industrial pensions to the employee of private persons, whose labor has largely either gone to the profit of these employers, or been worse than wasted in competitive and other economically useless lines of labor, is not good economics. It partakes of the unscientific character of charitable enterprises, and if carried too far must end in bankruptcy of the public treasury. The application of the pension or guarantee of maintenance, also, to workers, should logically proceed pari passu, step by step, with the nationalizing of business. Although Germany and France have got the cart a little before the horse in this respect they are certain to discover their mistake by its effects. The idea of pensioning workers once having been established, the tax-payers are bound presently to see the necessity of protecting the treasury against loss by making the workers public employees, and so making sure that the public gets its money's worth. It is sure to be all one in the end whether a nation begins by nationalizing business or by pensioning the employees

of private businesses. The nationalizing of business, if
that comes first, will lead directly to pensioning the employees, while the pensioning of the employees of private businesses if that come first, is in the end equally
certain to lead to the public conduct of the businesses
themselves.

XIX

Talks on Nationalism—To a Disciple of Malthus

Mr. Smith, who has lately joined the nationalists, meets a disciple of Malthus, who fears that the comfortable conditions of life which nationalism will secure to all will result in too great an increase of population.

Disciple of Malthus:– I see only one objection to your plan.

Smith:– Well, if that is so, you can't be far from the kingdom of heaven.

Disciple of Malthus:– If that is what you call nationalism, I am afraid I am a good way from it, for though I have only one objection, it is a fatal one.

Smith:– What is it?

Disciple of Malthus:– Simply that, given the condition of society which you propose, the population of the world would multiply at such a rate as soon to press upon the possibilities of subsistence, the result of which would be universal famine.

Smith:– Why should population increase faster under nationalism than now?

Disciple of Malthus:– I understand that nationalism,

TO A DISCIPLE OF MALTHUS

while requiring service from every citizen, absolutely guarantees the maintenance of all.

Smith:– Certainly.

Disciple of Malthus:– That takes away all motive for prudence in having children. There will be no check upon natural impulse, and the result will be early marriages and a great increase of the birth rate, while, on the other hand, owing to the comfort and independence guaranteed the old, the sick and the crippled, and indeed all classes, the death rate will be greatly diminished. The result would be, no doubt, a great immediate increase in the world's sum of happiness, but in the end an overpopulation which would lead to a condition of greater ultimate misery than the present state.

Smith:– If I understand you rightly, your argument is that security as to maintenance for themselves and their offspring will lead people to marry earlier and have children more recklessly than they would if they were uncertain as to the future.

Disciple of Malthus:– That is indisputable, I think.

Smith:– Well, an ounce of fact is worth a ton of theory. In every community there is a wealthy class, the members of which feel a considerable degree of security as to their own future and their children's. Is it a fact that the wealthy classes have a larger number of children per family than the poorer classes? Is it the millionaire's wife or the laborer's which is most likely to have a dozen children?

Disciple of Malthus:– Undoubtedly the average size of the family is greater with the poor than the rich.

Smith:– I thought so. But, if that is so, what becomes of your theory? The well-to-do family today is in something like the position of prospective security in which all families will be under nationalism, while the millionaire's family enjoys a still higher degree of assurance for the future. There is no reason, so far as material conditions are concerned, why marriages among the rich should not take place at the earliest possible moment, or why there should be any limit to the number of children. In point of actual experience, however, the age of marriage is later and the number of children less, almost in proportion to the wealth of classes. On the other hand, in proportion as people are poverty-stricken they marry early and multiply recklessly. The conclusion seems to be that the way to overcrowd the world is to reduce the masses to a state of want stopping just short of famine, and, indeed the condition of the most densely populated regions of the world, China, portions of India and of Europe practically demonstrates that conclusion.

Disciple of Malthus:— But, it is said to be a statistical fact, in Europe at least, that the birth rate rises as the price of wheat falls, and certainly we know that there are more marriages in good times than in bad.

Smith:— Certainly, but the increase is among the poor or struggling class, and not among the well-to-do. The immediate results of temporarily improved circumstances are very different from the final results of permanently improved circumstances. Nationalism proposes not merely a temporary reduction in the price of wheat, but a permanent elevation of the masses to a condition of intelligence and comfort. When a poor man has a fortune left him, he may celebrate by going on a spree, but he ends by becoming as conservative as other rich men. Just so the first effect of such an improvement in the general condition of men might be a good deal of activity in marriages and births, as soon as the novelty of being able to be married at will wore off, the tendency to reckless matrimony would rapidly fall off to the very moderate degree of intensity which now marks it among the wealthy class. Did you ever stop to think why rich people are much less given to early marriages and large families than the poor and wretched?

Disciple of Malthus:– I don't know that I ever seriously considered the matter.

Smith:– Well, you should do so, for not only is the fact of the comparative abstinence of the well-to-do in this aspect a matter-of-fact refutation of your argument against nationalism, but the reason for the fact is a philosophical confirmation of that refutation. The reason the poor and ignorant classes are so dominated by the sexual impulse is the rudeness and narrowness of their lives, and the lack of the wide and numerous diversions of thought and interest which culture and refinement open to their possessors. In proportion as the mind and taste are developed, human beings are freed from bondage to the crude bodily appetites. The sexual passion is not indeed diminished in total intensity by intellectual and spiritual culture, but like light that passes through a prism, it is refracted into many shades and hues. There is still another reason, and a more important one than any I have yet referred to, why nationalism will not lead to over-population.

TALKS ON NATIONALISM

Disciple of Malthus:— What is that?

Smith:— Simply the fact that a corner-stone of nationalism is the absolute economical independence of women, whether married or unmarried, which means her complete bodily independence. Sex will no longer be a means of livelihood. Enforced maternity will be at an end. Neither by direct force nor the indirect coercion resulting from pecuniary dependence will women be made involuntary mothers. The tremendous influence of this new factor in human history cannot be over-estimated. In my opinion, the population of the world today is greater than it will ever be again. Far from tending to overcrowd the world, the general adoption of the principles of nationalism will, in my opinion, rather tend to diminish than to increase the number of the race, while constantly refining its quality.

XX

Talks on Nationalism—To a Neighbor

*Mr. Smith, who has joined the nationalists,
has a talk with a neighbor about the report-
ed invention of a flying-machine by Mr.
Maxim.*

Neighbor:– Did you read that account in the morning
paper of the flying-machine Hiram Maxim, the great
gun-maker, claims to have invented?

Smith:– Yes, I saw it.

Neighbor:– This is a wonderful age! We seem to
go faster and faster. Yesterday it was the steam-engine;
today it is electricity; tomorrow, air navigation. Maybe
Maxim has not succeeded so well as he claims; but if he
has not, somebody presently will. More wits are now
working at this problem than any other, except electricity,
and on more hopeful lines than ever before. The idea
of the flying-machine is in the air, and the machine itself will soon be.

Smith:– No doubt you are right. Probably it would
not be reckless to predict that a more or less complete
method of air navigation will be in use before many years.

Neighbor:– I would give more for the fame of the
inventor of the first successful flying-machine than for
that of Christopher Columbus. It will be the biggest

thing in human history, and the greatest single contribution to human welfare.

Smith:– It will undoubtedly lead to the accumulation of some vast fortunes.

Neighbor:– I speak of the general benefits to the race.

Smith:– I don't see where they would come in, as society is at present constituted.

Neighbor:– Why, man, by dispensing with roads and minimizing the need of motor power, air navigation would revolutionize transportation and abolish distance.

Smith:– So did the steam-engine; but what has that done for society?

Neighbor:– It has multiplied many fold the world's wealth.

Smith:– No doubt; but who has possession of that wealth? The steam engine has brought in the millionaire and is fast developing the billionaire. Perhaps air navigation will prepare the way for the trillionaire. At any rate, you may be sure that under the present industrial system it will simply prove another and yet more efficient device for enabling the capitalists to exploit the labor of the masses and levy toll upon their necessities.

Neighbor:– Oh, come now, you are too pessimistic by half.

Smith:– Well, see if I am. Let us look at the matter. I am not theorizing. The prediction that under the present industrial system the flying-machine would be no benefit to the masses is simply a plain deduction from history. It is about half a century since the steam-engine was generally applied to manufacturing and com-

124

TO A NEIGHBOR

merce. What is the result? As you say, there has been a prodigious increase in the world's wealth undoubtedly; but that wealth is in the hands of a few, and that few is constantly growing fewer, and their individual accumulations larger. It is the steam-engine which created and supports the plutocracy that today is strangling the republic. The sewing-machine was an invention with an evidently great potentiality for lightening the burdens of humanity, especially of women. It has enriched a number of individuals; but has it alleviated the condition of the masses? Go ask the victims of the sweat shops, and the sewing women of the great cities who work double hours for half a living. Within 10 years we have had the electric light and the telephone. They are wonderful inventions, truly, but what good have they done the people? Oppressive corporations, which are the tyrants of cities and states, have been based on them, but they have not by one jot or tittle relieved the misery of the world. The arc-light reveals scenes of squalor, misery and human degradation which the tallow candles of our fathers never witnessed.

Neighbor:– Then you think that it would have been better if all these inventions had never been made?

Smith:– No; because the people are going to destroy the plutocracy and replace the present slave system of industry by a co-operative organization of it. If I did not believe this, I should certainly say that the steam-engine and all other inventions which tend to the more effective concentration and organization of industry were bad. If these devices are to render that organization more efficient, chiefly in the interest of a few, as now,

125

they do but tend toward industrial tyranny worse than any ancient form of domination of man by man. Anarchy and carnage were better than that. But if they can be made, as we believe they can, by an industrial organization on the republican principle of a commonwealth, to promote the equal welfare of all, they will become unmitigated blessings to the race. Suppose, for instance, when the steam-engine had been introduced, there had already existed the equal industrial partnership of the people which nationalism proposes. Not only then would the wealth it produced have been equally shared, but it would have produced tenfold more wealth to be divided, for, under the system of industry which we propose, there could never be panics, crises or "over-production," but the wheels of manufacture would whir with an ever-swelling song; and not till leisure seemed to be equal partners of more worth than greater luxury would their music slacken.

XXI

Talks on Nationalism—To a Lover of Variety

Mr. Smith, who has lately joined the nationalists, meets a lover of variety in life.

Lover of Variety:– My objection to the system of society which you propose is that it would utterly destroy variety in life. The idea of a community in which everybody lived just the same way is intolerable to me.

Smith:– You have been misinformed if you think that everybody will live alike under nationalism.

Lover of Variety:– Why, under nationalism I thought everybody was to have the same income. Is not that so?

Smith:– Certainly; everybody will be an equal partner in the industrial organization of the nation, as he is now in its political organization, and will share its profits equally, as he now, nominally, does its political advantages.

Lover of Variety:– So I thought; and I ask you what is going to come of variety in life, when everybody has, let us say, just $3,000 income a year,—no more, no less. Why, they will become as like as peas.

Smith:– Then you think that the variety of life is

owing wholly to the difference in the amount of people's expenditure.

Lover of Variety:– It is not as much the difference in the amount of their expenditure as the different objects for which it is expended, that makes variety.

Smith:– That is nearer the truth, I think; and the different ways which people have of spending money are in turn interesting only because that is one of the ways in which differences of taste and temperament show themselves. It is this fundamental class of differences which makes society interesting. Well, in this respect I think we can suit you, under nationalism. People's tastes and temperaments will presumably differ then as much as now, and their modes of expenditure correspondingly. It is not likely that any two persons will be more likely to spend their income similarly under nationalism than now.

Lover of Variety:– Nevertheless I am sure that equality of incomes would tend to a tedious uniformity in modes of life.

Smith:– Well, fortunately, we don't need to theorize as to that question. We can put it to the test of practical experience. Now, there are Dick Rapid, Frank Prettyboy, George Pusher and yourself; your salaries are about the same, aren't they?

Lover of Variety:– They are the same to a penny, as I happen to know.

Smith:– Well, now, do you and Dick Rapid live alike? Is there a monotonous resemblance in your habits?

Lover of Variety:– I should say not.

TO A LOVER OF VARIETY

Smith:– Of course not. You are very properly offended by the suggestion. Dick spends his income on whiskey, fast horses and fast women; and you are a church member in good standing, with a wife and children. And yet, according to your theory as to the effect of equality of incomes under nationalism, you ought to be as much alike as peas in a pod. But take another case. Take Frank Prettyboy's case. Is there a tedious similarity between your modes of life?

Lover of Variety:– He is a dude, without a thought beyond his clothes, his eyeglass and his cane. He is a sissy.

Smith:– Dear me; why, this seems to be another case in which your theory does not closely correspond with facts. How about George Pusher? Is he—

Lover of Variety:– That'll do. I admit your point.

Smith:– Yes, I think you will have to admit that a pretty abundant variety in life is quite consistent with equality of incomes. Otherwise, you would get yourself into bad company.

Lover of Variety:– The fact remains, however, that, instead of many classes in society, you will have but one. Surely you will admit that a society is more interesting in which there is a variety of classes.

Smith:– To outsiders it may present a more interesting appearance, but to its members it will become uninteresting and unprofitable in precise proportion as it is split up into classes. By breaking up hard-and-fast class lines, based upon material conditions, and leaving the units to arrange themselves in mobile groups, according to affinities and without artificial obstacles, nation-

129

alism will incalculably increase the interest of human life. Social classes are prisons for their inmates, whether the bars be gilded, as in the case of aristocracies or "exclusive" sets, or the result of iron circumstance, as in the case of the laboring class. It is true that the so-called "exclusive" class builds its own prison and takes an incomprehensible pride in the strength of the bars through which it peers; but it is not the less the sufferer from being cut off from the body of humanity, than are the involuntary prisoners of poverty. Nationalism will break the bars and set the prisoners free, whether voluntary or involuntary. Could there be a more miserable spectacle than the stratification of society according to pecuniary income, which now exists? At the bottom comes the unskilled laborer class, with less than two dollars a day. Next an artisan class with three to four dollars a day. Then the small business and professional class, with a thousand to two thousand; and so on up, each class representing a miserable little world in itself, whose inhabitants really understand little and consequently care little about the rest of the world. Nationalism will end this inhuman condition of things, by smashing the whole formation, and leaving the atoms free to move among themselves, and assert their natural affinities.

Lover of Variety:– You are mixing your figures freely; prisons, strata,—what next?

Smith:– Only this more. Human society is like a great body of water. Cut it up into ponds and patches by dikes and dams, and it will turn stagnant, and breed only cat-fish and minnows. Throw down the dikes, and let the waters freely flow and mingle throughout their full extent, and they will grow sweet and clear, and nourish fish both big and healthy. Nationalism proposes to smash the dikes; and, if you really want more variety in life, you can't do better than take your shovel and help.

XXII

Talks on Nationalism—To a Collegian

Mr. Smith, who has joined the nationalists, meets a young collegian, who expects to graduate the next week.

Smith:— This is graduation week with you, I understand.

Collegian:— Yes, the class is launched on Thursday. The last prop is knocked out at noon, and then—ho, for the voyage of life!

Smith:— I hope it will be a long and successful one in your case.

Collegian:— I don't know about that. The annual newspaper editorials, which are printed along in the commencement season, credit us graduates with an overweening confidence in our abilities to go forth and conquer the world, but, so far as I know our men, that theory is a mistake. The fact is, while we keep a stiff upper lip, the most of us feel a little panicky over the prospect.

Smith:— I don't doubt it. I know I did, and if I had known what was before me, I confess I should have felt more panicky still.

Collegian:— You had a hard time, then?

Smith:— Perhaps not harder than most men, but hard

132

enough. I was 10 years knocking around from pillar to post before I found anything to do by which I could fairly support myself and think of having a family. I find plenty of men who have had the same experience. What are you going into?

Collegian:– There's the rub. I prefer the law, but I understand that the profession is desperately over-crowded, and there is little chance for a fellow who cannot get the business of some big corporation.

Smith:– I suspect that is just about true. How about medicine?

Collegian:– I've talked with a number of young doctors about practising medicine, but they all advise me to die some easier death. Really, they say that half the doctors of the country are living on half rations.

Smith:– How about the ministry?

Collegian:– No vocation for it. I suppose I shall try to get a little school-teaching and wait for something to turn up. There were a lot of the men up in my room last night, discussing our futures, and, except a few rich men's sons, we agreed that the outlook for the average college graduate, in the present crowded state of the professions, was drearier than it had ever been before. I've made up my mind that it would have been better if my poor father had not slaved so hard before his death to send me to college. I might have done something in business, perhaps.

Smith:– I don't think you need fret about any lost opportunity in that direction. If the professional men are crowding each other uncomfortably, the syndicates and trusts are crowding the business men out of existence. Every one of these business consolidations, with which the papers are full, fences up one more field of opportunity to independent business enterprise. A barber's shop will soon be about the only business a man can start without a big capital behind him.

Collegian:– I used to say that, if worst came to worst, I was strong enough to dig or heave coal for a living, but I see by the papers that there are a million unemployed workingmen in the country, and I'm afraid I should have to take my place at the end of a pretty long cue. In his baccalaureate, last Sunday, Prex got eloquent about the world's need of workers and the careers of usefulness that were just begging us to follow them. What rot! As a matter of fact, the world doesn't want any more workers, it has got too many already; too many lawyers, too many doctors, too many parsons, too many tradesmen, too many mechanics, too many day laborers. If a man is going to get a chance to work, whether to dig, teach, or cure people, he has to fight for it. I don't understand it. It is all a muddle. One would think that the world would welcome workers, for, after all, it is work that makes wealth.

Smith:– Look out, or you'll end by being a nationalist.

Collegian:– What has nationalism got to say about this?

Smith:– It says the last word and the only word in which there is any help. Under nationalism the world will welcome its workers. It will wait for them with eagerness, take careful account of their powers and bestir itself, with all possible solicitude, to find for each the place his tastes and powers best fit him for and to extend his field of usefulness as he shows ability to fill it.

Collegian:– Well, that's what we want; but why can't we have it now without nationalism! Surely, it is the general interest that all should find work.

Smith:– It is the general interest, but not the individual interest. Under the present system, the individual worker depends upon his particular earnings, not upon his share of the general earnings. His particular interest and the general interest are in direct contradiction. It is the general interest that all should be at work. It is the particular interest of every individual worker that as few as possible should work at his business, lest the demand for him and consequently his earnings should either be positively diminished or fail to increase as they otherwise might. This accounts for the discrepancy between the baccalaureate theory that the world wants workers and the difficulties placed in the way of everybody who tries to get work.

Collegian:– And what will nationalism do about it?

Smith:– It will identify the economical interest of the individual absolutely with that of the community, by making his income consist of an equal share of what the community makes, instead of consisting, as now, of what he can make out of the community. The result will be that every worker will be as eager to encourage other workers as he now is to discourage them; for every man not employed to the best advantage will be a loss to all.

Collegian:– I can see that everybody would be anxious to get everybody else at work under nationalism, but

135

what motive has he to work himself, since he will be provided for anyhow?

Smith:– The obligation to work at some business of mind or muscle would be a law as binding and unavoidable as military service under the German system, and open repudiation of it would, no doubt, be harshly dealt with. But really, I think the pains and penalties of the law would rarely need to be invoked. I imagine the man's comrades could be pretty safely trusted to see that he didn't loaf. I should be very sorry for a worker who, under such a system as nationalism, should get himself looked upon as a confirmed shirk. His experience, I fancy, would be something like that of an Indian youth who has got the reputation in his tribe of being a coward. A man who loafs, nowadays, is despised, but he hurts nobody in particular, and so is tolerated; but a loafer then would be recognized as a direct burden on every one of his fellows, and a thief of their earnings. No, I think that, what with public opinion in the foreground and the service law in the background, the community under nationalism would be less troubled with loafers than it ever was before.

Collegian:– But what is going to tempt a man to put forth his best efforts?

Smith:– The distinction and honors of the state, and the exercise of power.

Collegian:– Will that be motive enough without money?

Smith:– That is a funny question for a collegian. Is there any community on earth where emulation for distinction is more intense than in a university, and is there anywhere it is more wholly unaffected by money consideration?

Collegian:– No; that's a fact.

Smith:– It is far more intense, as well as more honorable in the school and university than in business life, because the money measure of effort and of talent is base, unfair and every way degrading. I fully believe that the sordid nature of the prizes set before men in mature life, under the present system, do more to discourage emulation than to encourage it, and that under nationalism we shall see honorable ambition become intensified as a motive, beyond any former experience.

XXIII

Talks on Nationalism—To a Banker

Mr. Smith, who has joined the nationalists, meets a banker who has heard that nationalism proposes to dispense with a circulating medium.

Banker:– You are going to get along without money in the good times coming, I hear. No use for men of my trade, eh?

Smith:– Use of the men, but none for their trade.

Banker:– Come now, is it actually a fact that you seriously look forward to a state of things here below when people will get along without money?

Smith:– Most assuredly.

Banker:– Well, well, I heard that you had some such idea, but I declare I wouldn't have believed, except on your own statement, that any set of men, outside of an asylum, believed it possible to abolish money. I suppose there is some sort of method in every sort of madness, and as you don't seem to be violent, I wish you'd tell me how you propose to go about it to abolish money. The only way you can prevent gold and silver from being used for money is to dump all there is in the world in the Atlantic ocean, and then put a guard over every mine in the world, to see that no more is obtained. I suppose something like that is your plan.

Smith:– Not at all. We have no idea of throwing away an ounce of metal.

Banker:– I see. You depend on some law strong enough, with penalties heavy enough, and policemen numerous enough back of it, to prevent people from circulating money by giving or accepting it for goods or services. You have taken a big job.

Smith:– Wrong again. There will be no need of any law on the subject. The people can be trusted not to circulate money without any legislation on the subject.

Banker:– Ah, that's it, then! You count on a great moral reform—a sort of a universal monetary total-abstinence pledge. It's a grand conception, but it won't work. The prohibitionists are rational compared with you. People can get on without whiskey, but not without money. The taste for alcohol is a mere whim compared with the auri sacra fames.

Smith:– Your suggestions are very ingenious, but none of them had occurred to us. We propose neither to destroy gold and silver, to forbid their circulation as money or to discourage it by moral means.

Banker:– Then, how on earth do you expect to prevent the use of money?

Smith:– We don't expect to prevent it; money will be disused because it will have become useless. Why are you willing to give a man a piece of your property or do him a service in exchange for a ten-dollar gold piece? Is it not because you know that the coin will enable you at any time to obtain the property or service of others?

TALKS ON NATIONALISM

Banker:– Of course.

Smith:– Suppose you knew, on the contrary, that the coin would not enable you to obtain anything either in the form of goods or services, would you take it?

Banker:– Naturally, I wouldn't.

Smith:– Very good. That will be the situation under nationalism. All production will be carried on by the nation, all public services will be maintained by it and private services, such as medical treatment, housework, etc., can only be obtained by application through the public administration. You will therefore have to apply to the nation for whatever goods or services you need. Gold, silver or money of any sort will not, however, be received by the nation, or in any way recognized as a tender. According to the plan of nationalism, the relation between the nation and the individual is not a commercial but a moral relation; not a relation of exchange but of reciprocal duties, the duty of maintenance on the part of the nation, and of service on the part of the citizen. As a citizen, you are entitled to an equal share of the total national product for the year in the form of a definite amount of wealth, to be utilized according to your wishes. Money is simply irrelevant to such a relation. It has nothing whatever to do with it. The present form of society is based on the value of things, not of men. Nationalism considers only the man. What does the value of gold or silver indicate as to the desert of its possessor? He may have stolen it, inherited it, found it by chance or obtained it in a hundred ways having certain relation with right and justice. Under nationalism, a man who, desiring to obtain something more than his equal share as a citizen, should offer a ton of gold, would simply be stared at; I doubt if he would even be arrested for attempted bribery.

Banker:– I should think that at least he would be arrested on that charge.

Smith:– Well, possibly he might be, but it would be difficult to convict him of having offered a valuable consideration.

Banker:– But surely the intrinsic value of gold would always remain, even if its value as money were taken away.

Smith:– No doubt, for ornament and in the arts, gold will always have some value, but even for these purposes it is chiefly sought and chiefly prized because its money quality lends it peculiarly the effects of luxury and ostentation. Once permanently destroy its value for money, as nationalism will do, and the demand for it for ornamental purposes will very greatly fall off. Gold ornaments will pass out of fashion.

Banker:– Well, granting, for the sake of the argument, that money might be dispensed with if nationalism were brought to pass, what does the admission amount to? Nationalism is impossible.

Smith:– We will discuss that some other time. The subject is a large one. But, certainly, if a co-operative industrial organization of the people upon the basis of the national organism and the economical equality of citizens be at all possible, the disuse of money must follow as a logical result, simply because there would be, in that case, no function left for a medium of exchange. Many of the critics of nationalism, like yourself, have referred to the disuse of money as the most absurd proposition of the nationalist programme. That is simply because they have not stopped to think. The disuse of money will be a necessary and inevitable result of nationalism, which will require no law for its enforcement but will necessarily result from the new industrial and social conditions. We do not aim to make new laws, but to establish new conditions which shall dispense with the need of laws.

XXIV

Talks on Nationalism—To a Prohibitionist

Mr. Smith, who has joined the nationalists, meets a prohibitionist.

Prohibitionist:– There is no doubt that your party is the coming party, on one condition.

Smith:– And that is—

Prohibitionist:– A prohibition plank in your platform.

Smith:– I confess I don't see how you make out that a prohibition plank would strengthen any party. According to the test of elections, which, within the past five years, have pretty well sampled the sentiment of north, south, east and west, the prohibition idea is on the wane.

Prohibitionist:– I admit that the elections have been against us; but the principle is the only right one, and the people are bound in the end to come around to it.

Smith:– If the principle is right, no doubt they will; but while we wait for that, there are many great abuses of the liquor business which ought to be corrected.

Prohibitionist:– The business is altogether an abuse. The only way to correct its abuses is to abolish it wholly.

Smith:– But how are you going to abolish it in states which refuse by great majorities to do so? The only way by which you can abolish it, in most parts of the union, at present, is by substituting minority for majority rule. You cannot seriously expect to do that.

Prohibitionist:— These are considerations of mere expediency. The liquor traffic is a crime, and it is a crime to compromise with it.

Smith:— Correcting the abuses of a business which you cannot abolish is not compromising with it, by any means. Don't you see that refusing to compromise, as you call it, with the liquor business, amounts to surrendering unconditionally to it? By taking up the attitude you do, you virtually exclude yourselves from participation in any remedial measures now practicable, or likely to be in the near future. Doesn't that seem a great pity?

Prohibitionist:— Perhaps there would be something in that argument if a generation of experiment in correcting the abuses of the traffic had not resulted in complete failure. The statute books of our state for thirty years are lumbered with the records of such experiments, and the net result has been nothing.

Smith:— I admit that the success of the efforts thus far in that line has been poor enough.

Prohibitionist:— Then why do you wish to continue the same line of policy?

Smith:— We do not. We propose a wholly new policy. The corrective liquor legislation of the past in this country has chiefly consisted in a series of pecuniary impositions upon dealers and petty persecutions of their customers, which have only exasperated both. The personal persecutions of the dealers has led to their being regarded by their patrons as a sort of heroes, while the pecuniary impositions by fines and licenses have led to an adulteration of liquors (for the purpose of recouping legal fines) which has been ruinous to the health of the people.

Prohibitionist:– That is all true; but what is this new sort of corrective system which you propose?

Smith:– We propose to entirely eliminate the motive of private greed in promoting intemperance, by putting the liquor business exclusively under public management.

Prohibitionist:– Nationalizing it, that is to say?

Smith:– Well, I suppose the first step would be to put the distributive or retail business under state and local management, leaving the business of production to be conducted by the nation when it got ready, for nationalization must necessarily wait till a majority of the entire nation favors it.

Prohibitionist:– That is to say, you propose to have the government turn rumseller.

Smith:– Precisely. Do you see any objection to a municipality selling the water to a community?

Prohibitionist:– Water is harmless.

Smith:– Certainly; and that is why it's sale might, so far as any moral reason is concerned, be safely left to individuals. Liquor is not harmless, and therefore it is not safe to leave its sale to individuals. It is exactly because rum is the dangerous thing it is that its distribution, seeing that it cannot be prevented, ought to be in public hands.

Prohibitionist:– It would be a pretty spectacle to see the government making a profit out of the vices of the people.

145

TALKS ON NATIONALISM

Smith:– Not so fast. It is a principle of nationalism that when the people, through their agents, assume charge of a business, they should not make a profit out of it beyond the expense and (during the transition stage to complete nationalism) so much more as may take the place of the taxes previously levied on the business, when it was in private hands. Consequently, the government would conduct the liquor business at cost. That means it would have absolutely no motive to encourage sales or to promote trade in any way. Would not this change be likely to result in a tremendous reduction in the amount of liquor consumed?

Prohibitionist:– I am bound to say that it would.

Smith:– Here is another point. Bad whiskey is as much worse than good, as good whiskey is more dangerous than water; and at present a large proportion of both spirituous and malt liquors are adulterated or improperly made. The liquors supplied for medicinal purposes by the majority of drug stores are often so bad as to be dangerous to the sick, a fact for which the druggists are by no means necessarily to blame, but rather the dealers who supply them. Now, under public management, all liquors supplied would be of official test and pure.

Prohibitionist:– There is something in that, no doubt.

Smith:– Well, then, here is another point. The law now forbids the sale of liquor to persons already intoxicated. If this law could be enforced, three fourths of the drunkenness on the streets, and the riotous disturbances resulting from it would be at an end. It never has been enforced, and cannot ever be, so long as liquor is sold for profit. It would end from the very day the

146

business passed into public hands. The salaried official, who had no interest in the business of the amount of sales, and would lose his place as the result of any disturbance traced to him, might be depended on to keep the safe side of the law. The same would be true of sales to minors. They would be at an end.

Prohibitionist:– As regards the public agencies, I admit that liquors would be likely to be sold by them strictly according to law, but what is to prevent unlicensed private persons from obtaining liquor and retailing it to any body who chose to buy, regardless of the law, as they do now?

Smith:– A business reason, much more effective than any law, would prevent it. The government agencies would sell at cost, and therefore could not be undersold. If people bought of the agencies to sell again, they could only make a profit by selling at an advance, which nobody would pay, especially as the goods would lack the government guarantee of quality. There have been various town-agency experiments in liquor selling before this, but they have chiefly failed from neglecting to adopt the nationalist principle of selling at cost. The result has been that unlicensed dealers have competed and beaten them, in spite of laws and penalties. Once let the state sell the best goods at cost and constables will be scarcely necessary to keep unlicensed dealers out of a business in which there would be no possible profit.

Prohibitionist:– Now you speak of it, I can see that this might have been why the old town-agency system did not work.

Smith:– That was one reason. Another was that it

147

was intended as a sort of prohibitory law in disguise. Everybody who purchased had to write his name down, and go through a regular inquisition. It was the policy of the law to discourage purchasers as much as possible. The result was that the customer would rather pay double price anywhere else than buy at the agency. Such a law could not help failing. Our plan is entirely different. It would not be disguised prohibition, but just what it pretended to be, merely the substitution of public and law-abiding management for private and law-breaking management. The state would do no more to discourage a buyer than to encourage him. There would be no writing down of names, or answering questions. Sales would be precisely as free as they now are in a licensed saloon, with the difference that the law would be absolutely complied with, as to the conditions of selling, and the condition of those to whom sales were made.

Prohibitionist:– And you would put these agencies into towns, whether they wanted them or not?

Smith:– On the contrary, the plan of public management need not interfere with local option. An agency need be put in only upon application of the municipality.

Prohibitionist:– One thing I like about the plan: it would abolish the saloon power in politics.

Smith:– It would certainly have that effect. I should judge that this would be enough to commend it to the prohibitionists.

Prohibitionist:– So far it would; but they will never abandon the prohibition idea.

Smith:– They need not. This plan is not proposed in place of prohibition, but in place of the present chaotic

148

and ruinous system. If the community ever gets ready for prohibition, public management will give place to it much more readily than the present system would, because there will be no private vested interests to antagonize the change. The question for you to answer is not whether public management promises better results than prohibition, which is at present impossible in most states, but whether it promises better results than the present system of private management for private profit.

Prohibitionist:— I am bound to admit that it certainly promises better results than those of the present system.

Smith:— Then it appears to me that you have no excuse for refusing to support it as the most genuine temperance measure at present in sight, especially as this is something you can do without in the slightest degree compromising your devotion to prohibition as an ultimate end.

Prohibitionist:— Under nationalism, I suppose, we should have complete prohibition?

Smith:— I don't know anything about that. We are none of us prophets. In my opinion, however, there will be a great deal more personal liberty under nationalism than now. You see, at present, a man's family is absolutely dependent on his conduct for maintenance, and therefore has a right to demand that he shall not bring them to want by bad habits. This right is the most foreible argument for prohibition. Under nationalism, women, whether married or unmarried, will be independent of men, holding, like men, a direct relation of duty and maintenance with the nation. So long, consequently, as a man's habits do not interfere with his service to

149

the nation, they will be strictly self-regarding in their consequences, and on that account there will be much less excuse for arbitrarily interfering with them than now. But, while I doubt whether the use of alcoholic beverages will be wholly discontinued, I do believe that drunkenness will become practically unknown.

XXV

Talks on Nationalism—To an Advocate of Restricted Immigration

Mr. Smith, who has joined the nationalists, meets an advocate of Restricted Immigration.

Advocate of Restricted Immigration:- My reform comes before yours. There is no use at all trying to improve the condition of a nation unless you can put a stop to the stream of undesirable population from abroad. You might as well expect to purify a pond into which a sewer is all the time emptying its contents. If you succeed by your nationalism in making the condition of the American people better than it is, you will only be offering a higher premium to encourage the degraded of foreign lands to rush in to share your blessings. So I tell you that my reform comes first. You must begin by an effective restriction of undesirable immigration; that once secured, you may expect to get the benefit of a better economical regime, but not before.

Smith:- I believe pretty much all classes are agreed that a reasonable restriction of immigration which shall not bar out honest poverty, is desirable. The difficulty is, to enforce such a restriction.

Advocate of Restricted Immigration:- The present

law is not strict enough. I would have a double inspection, one of intending immigrants by our consuls abroad before they sail, and another at our ports of entry, and would only admit persons having passports from our consuls abroad.

Smith:– That plan is liable to some rather serious objections. Our consuls in Europe would have to depend almost entirely upon the local police and church authorities for information in regard to the record and character of intending emigrants. It would be impossible that they should do a great deal to personally look up cases. It is to be feared that under these circumstances, foreign governments would practically control emigration, and find in our consular system a convenient addition to their police service. They would be likely to see that young men owing military service and political suspects did not get passports, and that disreputable characters did. Many of our foreign consuls are indeed foreigners, and upon them the pressure of their governments would be stronger than that of ours. Moreover, consider how great would be the arbitrary power vested in the hands of consuls over the whole future destiny of fellow creatures, by the authority without appeal to refuse passports. How likely would such a situation be to lead to bribery and gross abuses of all sorts!

Advocate of Restricted Immigration:– I admit that this aspect of the matter had not occurred to me.

Smith:– But while the system you propose would be oppressive to well-meaning immigrants, it would scarcely avail to hinder the ill-meaning ones. You assume that immigrants will come in only at ports of entry. If that

152

were so, no doubt your plan would work, but it is not so. We have a land frontier of 3,000 miles on one side and of 1,000 on the other. If you should have such an ironclad law as you want, it would simply result in the immigrants without passports landing at Montreal or Halifax, and coming across the border. This is already being extensively done, and to prevent it would require a picket line of police 3,000 miles long.

Advocate of Restricted Immigration:- Is there then no way by which we can protect ourselves from this deluge of criminals, paupers and barbarians.

Smith:- Something can be done no doubt by the enforcement of our present inspection laws and above all by the rigid punishment of the offending steamships. The evasion of the law by crossing the border cannot be prevented short of a universal passport system obligatory upon all citizens, by which people who have come in without passports might be at any time afterwards detected, and this would be an intolerable burden on the whole nation. A plan which in my opinion would be very efficacious is for the government to flood Europe with posters and advertisements contradicting the lying announcements of the immigration agents with statements as to the difficulty of obtaining employment here. A large portion of our immigrants come here as dupes, and if they knew the truth would stay at home. However, all these measures are mere make-shifts. Nationalism offers the only possible plan by which a nation can make sure of determining who shall and who shall not become a part of it. Laws to restrict immigration will be rendered needless by nationalism.

Advocate of Restricted Immigration:– How is that?

Smith:– Simply because under nationalism all the industries and means of production in the country will be under public control, and the workers will have access to them and to their products only as members of the organized industrial force. Except as they become enrolled as members of that force, there will be no means of livelihood open to them.

Advocate of Restricted Immigration:– That is to say there will be no more immigration whatever.

Smith:– Oh, not at all. There will be more reason to encourage desirable immigrants than there now is, for under nationalism there will be no competition for employment as now, but work for unlimited hands. The new system will be as advantageous for the immigrant as for the nation, for instead of having to seek for work in a strange land, he will be at once provided with a place, and an assured support; but on the other hand, no undesirable peron could possibly find means of livelihood.

Advocate of Restricted Immigration:– But can't a man emigrate unless as a worker? Is there to be no more travel or residence in foreign lands for pleasure and instruction?

Smith:– More than ever before no doubt. I spoke merely of the conditions on which alone an immigrant might find work and obtain a livelihood. If he has his livelihood already provided for in the form of credit earned at home, he has simply to exchange it into American credit, and live here on it at leisure as long as it lasts, the account being adjusted by international exchange.

154

XXVI

Talks on Nationalism—To a Favorably Disposed Person

Mr. Smith, who has joined the nationalists, meets a favorably disposed person, who, however, would like to have less said about making everybody economically equal.

Smith:– Why don't you join us? You seem to be favorably disposed toward Nationalism.

Favorably Disposed Person:– Yes, I don't mind saying that I am. In fact, between you and me I'm getting to be a pretty good nationalist. The truth is, according to the way things are going now, I don't see anything, unless it be nationalism, that is going to save the country from everlasting smash within ten years. There is one thing I'm not quite ready for though, and I think you would be wise if you did not make it quite so prominent in your propaganda.

Smith:– What is that?

Favorably Disposed Person:– Your doctrine of economical equality, that is to say, that the provision made for all is to be the same. A good many, like myself, are quite ready to go in for the other features of nationalism, but are not prepared for this.

Smith:– Of course not. Nobody is. I am sure you

never heard a nationalist advocate the application of that principle under the present industrial conditions. It necessarily presupposes the complete nationalization of industry, and can only be fully introduced when that has been accomplished.

Favorably Disposed Person:– But why should it be introduced at all? Why should it be regarded as a necessary feature of nationalism?

Smith:– It ought not to be very difficult to make you see that. What is it we nationalists propose? We ask a republican nation to substitute for the present individualistic industrial system, a national partnership for the organization of industry and the distribution of its products. Now these people are already political copartners, and as political copartners they are asked to ordain, establish and continuously to maintain the proposed industrial partnership, which must rest upon the political organization. As political copartners they are equals. Is anybody so exceedingly simple as to suppose that these equal political partners will consent to become parties to an unequal industrial partnership? Look at it another way. Nationalism proposes that the national organization, hitherto merely political, be extended over the industrial field. The principle of the national political organization is one of absolute equality; is it likely that in extending the national organization its fundamental principle will be abandoned? Why, my dear fellow, there are many ideas on the possible developments of nationalism, on which there is room for difference of opinion, but as to its being characterized by an equal law of service and an equality of distribution, there is not the slightest.

TO A FAVORABLY DISPOSED PERSON

That equality will be the law of the new nation is pre-determined by the fact that it will be the work and will of a people who are already political equals.

Favorably Disposed Person:– That is a point I had not thought of. You claim, then, that quite apart from any questions whether or not, philosophically speaking, economical equality ought to be the law of nationalism, it must be so, owing to the preexisting and predetermining political conditions in this country.

Smith:– That is precisely it. The trouble with the people who object to economical equality as a feature of nationalism is that they approach the subject from the point of view of the socialists, which is European and suggested by European conditions, instead of from the point of view of the nationalists, which is American and suggested by American conditions. According to the socialists, the coming order will be chiefly a result of social and industrial evolution as distinguished from political and national evolution. Granting the accuracy of this view, the coming social order might conceivably be variously organized as to the principle of equality. Nationalists, however, declare that the evolution of the new order, while affected and promoted by social and industrial evolution, is primarily a political and national evolution, the first step of which is logically the establishment of a political republic, with the subsequent extension to the industrial organization of society of the principle of equality already established in the political organization. A new industrial system emerging directly from an aristocratical or monarchical society might recognize and perpetuate inequalities; but established by a republican nation, it must be founded upon the principle of equality. Therefore, whether or not economical equality should characterize socialistic regimes which might be established in Europe, it must inevitably be the foundation of any new industrial system established in America. In one sense, there would be no objection to dropping the talk about economical equality as the goal of nationalism; it would not make a particle of difference about the result. But in another and more important respect, it would be suicidal, for it would kill the soul of nationalism, which is the principle of human brother-hood—the enthusiasm of humanity.

Favorably Disposed Person:– That's very pretty; but is it fair? After all, should a man not have what he produces, even though it means that some have more than others? Justice before generosity.

Smith:– By all means, justice. There never yet was any generosity, for no man ever gave or could give all he owed. We owe all we are. Has not a mother a right in the strength of her son, and if a mother, then has not the great mother—humanity—an infinitely greater right? It makes me laugh to hear a man who is himself a product, claiming that he has a right to all he produces, and to nothing more. If that be so, he has no right to himself. His phrase shuts his own mouth. The only way a man may excuse himself for enjoying this earth and his own life is by the perpetual tribute of a social duty measured only by his gifts.

Favorably Disposed Person:– I will not say you are not right. I know in my heart that you are; in fact, your whole talk is a gross plagiarism from the New Testament.

TO A FAVORABLY DISPOSED PERSON

But I am pretty conservative; in fact, it is my conservatism which, in face of the present ruinous tendency of business, has made me a nationalist, and I confess that the idea of a universal economic equality is rather startling.

Smith:- You must remember that it is no more and probably less startling to you, than the idea of the right of all men to an equal share in political administration was to your great grandfather. The world's precedents, save here and there a brief and ill-starred experiment, had been of kingly right and aristocratic leadership. Now, suddenly it was proposed that men should share power equally—the sage with the ploughman, the wealthiest with the poorest, the warrior with the cripple, the lord of a thousand acres with the humblest tenant. Your present scare ought to enable you to sympathize with your ancestors, for really that experiment was far bolder than this. And yet, who would wish it retracted? Even as you laugh at the terrors of your ancestors, in presence of the spectre of political equality, will our children laugh at the alarm of their parents at the advent of equality in the social sphere.

XXVII

Talks on Nationalism—To a Successful Business Man

Mr. Smith, having joined the Nationalist Club, is buttonholed by a friend, who is a successful business man, with the following result:—

Successful Business Man:— What's this I hear, Smith? They tell me you've joined those lunatics who call themselves nationalists; I always thought you were a man of sense.

Smith:— You have been mistaken all the while, then. I never was a man of sense till I joined the nationalists.

Successful Business Man:— Oh, come, now; do you suppose if all the world's wealth were to be divided equally, as you nationalists propose, that it would be 10 days before some men had doubled their pile and as many more had lost theirs?

Smith:— I am afraid you do not know what you are talking about. Nationalists don't want either a general divide or a partial one; in fact, they would be more strongly opposed to a division than any other class of people, and on more logical grounds. Their chief objection to the present system is that it is based on dividing among individuals what is rightfully an estate in

160

common, and one to which men can have no valid title
except in common. What they propose is an ownership
in common of the world's capital and a general partnership for carrying on the business.

Successful Business Man:– Of course you know that
is nothing more nor less than rank communism!

Smith:– Very true, if you call a business partnership communism. In a business partnership the capital
is held in common, and the income only divided; and that
is exactly what we propose. If you and your partners
in the woolen business are communists, why, then the
nationalists are; if not, why, they are not,—for they
merely propose to extend the partnership principle to the
whole business of the world.

Successful Business Man:– The cases are not parallel.
My woolen business may be communism, strictly speaking, but there are a good many differences between that
sort of partnership and the plan you propose. I pick
the men I want to go in partnership with. They put in
as much money as I do and as much work, and if we
disagree we can dissolve at any time. Your proposed
partnership, on the other hand, is universal, involuntary
and indissoluble, except by a revolution. It is a sort
of partnership for which there isn't any precedent.

Smith:– Oh, yes, there is. You are a member of just
such a partnership at this moment and always have been.
As an American you belong involuntarily to a partnership indissoluble, except by revolution. You have 65,-
000,000 copartners, not one of whom you picked out.
The amount of capital they have invested in the business
varies from $200,000,000 to nothing at all, and yet all the

partners have an equal voice in voting away the property and even the lives of the copartners. Do you object to this copartnership? Would you like to get out of it?

Successful Business Man:– I am not prepared, on the whole, to say that I would, though certainly it has a great many drawbacks.

Smith:– Exactly. It has a great many drawbacks, and these drawbacks can only be remedied by adopting the nationalist plan. The faults of the present national partnership largely result from the fact that the partners, while having all equal voice, have very unequal investments. This inequality prevents a sense of a common interest on the part of the partners, and without that no partnership can be successful. Nationalism, by equalizing the stake in the country held by all the partners, will create an absolute community of interest as to its management, and thus render democratic government in practice the admirable system which hitherto it has been only in theory.

Successful Business Man:– That may be all very pretty in the way of theory, but in practice such a plan would break down completely. Under the present system lazy folks won't work, but under yours, not even naturally industrious ones would. How are you going to induce a man to do his best if he is to get no more income than the man who does just enough to avoid punishment as an idler? Do you suppose I'd have worked as I have if I knew I should never have any more money than the fellows around me who loafed?

Smith:– Most certainly I do. It would have tired you as much to be lazy as it would a lazy man to be industrious. Nobody is ever made energetic except in a brief and spasmodic way by incentives from without. All motive power worth taking account of works from within. A man is like a locomotive: the power that makes him go is inside. If the power is weak, he can't be made to go. If he is strong, he must go or blow up.

Successful Business Man:– I suppose there is something in that, but a man is not quite like an engine, after all. He wants some sort of a reward to work for.

Smith:– Of course, he does and nationalism will hold out far stronger inducements to diligence than the present system does, because its whole plan will make rank and official position, from the foreman to the president, depend solely upon achievement in the public service. Rank won in this way will be a far more absolute measure of merit than gold, which is as likely "to gild the straitened forehead of the fool," or crown rascality as to reward industry. The nationalist plan will open the career to talent as it never was opened before. Under it men of force and energy will find their place and reap the rewards of their qualities as they never did before.

Successful Business Man:– But not in cash.

Smith:– No, certainly not in cash. But don't imagine that you will miss it. Apart from its necessity as a guarantee of comfort, which will then be a matter of course, the pride you have in your money is as a means of position and power and a proof of success in life. The same amount of energy expended under nationalism will even more surely bring you position and power, which will in turn be far more obvious and brilliant proofs of success in life than the biggest of bank accounts. The fact is, my dear fellow, all you successful business men are unlucky in having been born before your time. You would have had a far better chance if you could have waited for nationalism.

Successful Business Man:– Well, well, you have it bad, haven't you? Of course I should be pleased, on account of your friends, if you could convince me that you are not so badly cracked as I think you are. But I can't stop now. I am due at a creditors' meeting in a case of bankruptcy. One thing your friends the nationalists have got dead rights, I'll admit: something queer is the matter with business.

XXVIII

Talks on Nationalism—To a Pastor

Mr. Smith, who has recently joined the Nationalist Club, meets his pastor.

Pastor:– You are just the man I wanted to have a chat with. I understand that you've joined the Nationalist club, and probably you can tell me something about nationalism. People are discussing it, and I was thinking of preaching a sermon on it. If I do, I want to get my facts a little nearer right than some of my brethren have.

Smith:– I shall be very glad to tell you anything I know, but why don't you join the club and learn all about it? There are three or four ministers with us, so you wouldn't be lonely.

Pastor:– Ah, but I'm not quite ready for that. I'm afraid there are some rather fundamental differences in the way we look at this question of perfecting society. If I understand you nationalists correctly, you expect to make men perfect by improving their environment, while it is the Christian doctrine that if you reform the individual, social reform will follow. You say abolish the wage system; but Christ says, "Ye must be born again."

Smith:– Well, why not both? Is there anything inconsistent between Christianity and the bettering of men's environment? Would it be a good answer to an inquirer who was advocating an improved system of sanitation that he ignored the necessity of personal piety? Really, my dear sir, it is totally incomprehensible to me why you should fancy that in insisting on the need of personal reformation you are in opposition to nationalism. We agree fully to all you or anybody else can say on that theme; but we call attention to the fact that to improve society, not only a good heart but a good plan is necessary.

Pastor:– My remark was, I suppose, suggested by having heard nationalism spoken of as a sort of new religion.

Smith:– It is a religion most emphatically, but it is not a new religion. It is the religion Christ taught. It is applied Christianity. It is Christ's doctrine of the duty of loving one's neighbor as one's self, applied to the reorganization of industry.

Pastor:– It seems to me there are two sides to that argument. If you are engaged in applying Christianity to society, why, so is the church. Seeing, then, that we are engaged in the same work, why should not you nationalists turn to and help the church through its agencies, especially seeing that the church is already in the field?

Smith:– Because the reorganization of society which is needed to render Christianity possible is an industrial and economic reorganization, which the church as such has hitherto declined to take hold of.

Pastor:– But is it so certain that an industrial reorganization is needed for society? May not the church, in dwelling chiefly upon the necessity of personal reformation, be taking the surest though the slowest way to perfect the social condition? You will surely admit that if every one lived a truly godly life, the industrial problem would disappear.

Smith:– Oh, my dear sir, it seems that you could scarcely make a more vital or complete mistake than this. Go on, by all means, and do all you can to promote personal goodness; but do not delude yourself with the idea that any amount of moral reformation can solve a problem which in basis is essentially economic. If every man on earth were a saint, if all fraud and intentional wrong-doing were banished from business, the moral evils of the business system would indeed be removed; but the fatal economic defects would remain; and, although men would be happier, because better, they would be well-nigh as poor as now. You would think a farmer a fool who would expect to make a living by a bad and wasteful system of husbandry merely because he was a truly good man. But even if it were true that universal moral reform would solve the industrial problem, could you candidly hold out much hope of its being accomplished within any near or calculable time?

Pastor:– I am afraid I could not.

Smith:– Well, I can. You good men who have a little suspicion of nationalism as a plan to side-track Christianity will recognize, when you shall sufficiently consider the matter, that it aims to clear away obstacles which have hitherto hindered the progress of Christianity and will open to it a career such as the imagination of a saint never pictured. The trouble with the present competitive system of business is that it will not let a man be good, though he wants to. So long as it shall remain, your ministry is destined to be in the main futile. Pardon me; but it is mockery to tell men to live by the ethics of Jesus to-day. The law you lay down for them the necessities of their wives and children plead with them to disobey, and they do disobey, and let him who is blind blame them. My eyes are at last opened, and I can do so no longer.

Pastor:– I feel how true that is. I have that feeling often enough; too often, I sometimes think, for my pastoral efficiency. I will say, Mr. Smith, that you have set some things before me in a new light. I am not quite yet ready to join your club, but I will admit that I am glad that I did not preach that sermon on nationalism before we had this talk. If you are right, the Christian church ought to be in this thing.

Smith:– The Christian church is bound to be in it just so far as it is Christian, and I do not mean to say that the bulk of its members are not sincere according to their light. This world-wide movement for social reconstruction on a higher plane, of which nationalism is a phase, is an infinitely greater thing than the anti-slavery movement; and while the slowness of the church to take the right side on that issue was a blow to its prestige in America from which it has not yet recovered, its failure to take the right side in this far vaster movement would not leave any church worth mentioning. Mind you, I don't say that it would leave no Christianity. The spirit of Christianity is imperishable and if the church failed would find other embodiments. But I do not believe the church will fail. There are a thousand cheering signs that its leaders will not be found sleeping at this new coming of the Son of Man.

XXIX

Talks on Nationalism—To Mrs. A.

Mr. Smith, who has joined the nationalists, meets an old friend, Mrs. A., who raises divers points in regard to the relations of nationalism with the servant question.

Smith:— You look tired out. Evidently you have had a hard day's shopping.

Mrs. A.:— I can assure you I have been engaged in a task much less pleasing than shopping. I've been servant hunting. Really, Mr. Smith, if you could only offer some solution of the servant question, the ladies would all become nationalists immediately.

Smith:— It would certainly be a confession of the insufficiency of our plan if we could not, for it claims to be a complete theory for the reconstruction of all industrial relations.

Mrs. A.:— I suppose you propose to solve the servant question under nationalism by abolishing servants altogether. Everybody being as good as everybody else, of course nobody will be willing to serve the others.

Smith:— On the contrary, everybody being the recognized equal of everybody else, there will be no more humiliation in serving others than you feel in pouring tea for your guests or waiting on tables at a charity fair.

169

As exercised between equals, service is the most graceful of human activities and always has been so considered. To serve is degrading only when and so far as it implies personal dependence and social inferiority. Under nationalism there will certainly be no servants in the sense of people whom you can order about roughly, scold, and treat with discourtesy; but of service, better, kinder, and more efficient than people ever yet received from one another, an abundance. As there will be then no serfs of poverty to lay the dirty work off upon, it will be the common interest to reduce its amount and disagreeableness to the utmost, and what must be done will be shared equally at some time of life, by all.

Mrs. A.:– That is a pleasant picture, but dear me, it is far off. Can't you give us some solution of the servant-question which shall help us a little now?

Smith:– I don't think that need be difficult. Did you ever consider what the difference is between domestic service and other sorts of work in shops, mills, etc., which makes girls so much prefer them to housework, although that is often so much easier?

Mrs. A.:– It has always seemed to me a very unreasonable preference on their part.

Smith:– I know it is customary to so regard it, but I think it can be easily shown that the preference is a very natural and even praiseworthy one. Domestic service is the only sort of work now left in the whole range of industries, in which there is a distinct implication of social inferiority on the part of the employer to the employee. It is not for nothing that the word "servant," which was formerly and still in many old-world countries is applied to all sorts of employees, is now in this country retained only for persons employed in domestic work. The mill owner or store proprietor may grind down the girls in his employ to half the wages of the house-servant and abuse them in all sorts of ways, but he does not think of calling them his servants nor would they endure it. Is it strange that girls of spirit prefer almost any hardship to taking employment in housework? Wouldn't you?

Mrs. A.:– Well, if you put it that way, I suppose I should.

Smith:– As if for the express purpose of making the position of houseworker still more impossible to a man or woman with any self-respect, has come of late the importation of European devices for emphasizing the servile position of house-workers by compelling them to wear badges of servitude in the way of caps, costumes, liveries, etc., which serve no possible end save that of ministering to the arrogance of employers and wounding the self-respect of those compelled by poverty to accept employment at any terms.

Mrs. A.:– Really, your words are rather hard.

Smith:– Are they any too hard? It seems to me that to wound the dignity and humiliate the self-respect of one's dependents is every whit as brutal as it would be to assault them with bodily blows. The ladies who are engaged in introducing these European inhumanities ought to be in better business. Really, when you think of it, the wonder is not that good domestics are so hard to secure but that there are to be found any persons at all who are willing to accept the humiliating conditions of the house-worker. American girls for a generation past have struck absolutely against this sort of conception and if it had not been for foreign immigration, the spirit of republicanism would long ago in this country have compelled a radical reformation of domestic service, which by abolishing the idea of the social inferiority of the employee would have placed it in line with other industrial occupations.

Mrs. A.:– I confess I don't see how that could be done. The conditions of housework are peculiar. The necessary intimacy, which the houseworker, although neither friend nor guest, has with the family, seems to make it necessary that she shall be conventionally regarded as occupying a socially distinct position.

Smith:– That difficulty suggests the way in which the reform will begin, which will probably be the abandonment of the idea of residence under the same roof of employer and employed. The house-worker will come from without, being furnished by establishments for that purpose, to perform specific duties or to work for certain periods at a certain rate just as the plumber or the carpet layer does now, and will have the same independence.

Mrs. A.:– Do you think that plan of service from outside would work?

Smith:– Of course it would work. Could anything possibly work worse than the present system, against the utter worthlessness of which every housekeeper is crying out more bitterly year by year? The notion that servility and obsequiousness on the part of the employee to the employer, which in these days is seen in no other department of industry should for some mysterious reason be indispensable when it comes to making beds and sweeping rooms, is utter nonsense. It is this studious effort to preserve the traditions of feudalism in the kitchen long after they have been supplanted by democracy and at least nominal equality in the workshop and the field, that accounts for the demoralized state of household work. The conditions of household service today are an anachronism. Modernize it, democratize it, and it may possibly last until nationalism comes, instead of breaking down midway, as it now seems liable to.

XXX

Talks on Nationalism—To a Prevention of Cruelty Man

Mr. Smith, who has joined the nationalists, meets a Society-for-the-Prevention-of-Cruelty-to-Animals Man.

Smith:– See here, didn't you know you were a nationalist?

Prevention of Cruelty Man:– I hadn't heard it before, and I don't believe it now.

Smith:– I thought you were interested in preventing the abuse of animals.

Prevention of Cruelty Man:– Well, so I am. What has nationalism to do with that?

Smith:– We propose a system of national co-operative industry which will abolish poverty and make it possible for men to live together in a humane and kindly manner.

Prevention of Cruelty Man:– That is all very well for the men, but how do the beasts come into the benefits of the arrangement?

Smith:– Because the condition of the beast depends absolutely upon the character and condition of its owner. The beasts are, after all, the greatest sufferers from poverty. It is always the weakest that the burden finally rests on. The corporation discharges an employee; he gets drunk, goes home and beats his wife; she whips the children, and they go out and stone the cat. Take the case of horses, for instance; I suppose the sufferings of the horse will be the largest single count in the indictment of the beasts against man on the day of judgment.

Prevention of Cruelty Man:— Undoubtedly.

Smith:— Well, what is it that is accountable for the greatest amount of the sufferings of the horse? Is it not the poverty of their owners? Why are horses overworked, overdriven, worked in old age, worked to death? Is it not owing to the stress of the struggle of existence felt by those who own them and have to use them for a livelihood, or, where it is not thus excusable, is it not the result of greed of gain? Nobody, save here and there some abnormal exception, abuses animals for the mere love of it. The horse of the well-to-do man is always well cared for and quite likely to be made a cosset of.

Prevention of Cruelty Man:— Yes; so long as he is in his prime. Then your rich man sells him off to the ragman or the scavenger for $10, to be clubbed to death.

Smith:— Precisely. Some men are mean enough for that, but they won't be able to do it under nationalism, for there will then be no such class of people for our rich to sell their leavings to. What is not good enough for one man to drive will not then be considered good enough for another man to drive. I tell you all the horses are nationalists. I was told so confidentially, by old Dobbin, only last night, when I was bedding him. He intimated that the news was getting around among the cattle, pigs and sheep, and we might count on them too, when we get ready to move.

Prevention of Cruelty Man:– What are you going to promise them?

Smith:– Poor creatures! at least an easy ending. We shall save them from being tortured to death. Take the matter of the transportation of cattle and other animals for food, there has been, and is, a horrible amount of cruelty in that business.

Prevention of Cruelty Man:– Enough to call down God's judgment on the earth.

Smith:– You are right, indeed. What has been the motive of the cruelties practiced by the transportation companies? It has been the desire to make the utmost possible money out of the business, and to waste as little as possible on humane contrivances and provisions. There have been, however, a number of ameliorating features introduced of late years. How have they been introduced?

Prevention of Cruelty Man:– By laws enacted under pressure of public opinion.

Smith:– Precisely. The people, acting through the government upon the corporations, have compelled, in that roundabout way, some improvements, in spite of the selfish greed of the corporations. Now, when the government conducts the meat-supply business as we nationalists want to have it, not only will public opinion operate directly to control its methods, but, moreover, in so operating it will have to contend with no selfish sentiment of greed on the part of the government, which will act merely as an agent.

TO A PREVENTION OF CRUELTY MAN

Prevention of Cruelty Man:– There is something in that.

Smith:– There is so much in it that I am very sure your society has only to take the matter under consideration to recognize whatever may be thought by it as to the abolition of the competitive system in general, that there is no way of putting an end to the horrors of the cattle car, except government management of the meat-supply business with the direct responsibility to public opinion which that would imply.

Prevention of Cruelty Man:– Actually, I don't see any other way of getting at it so directly. Do you know, I am quite interested in this notion of protecting the animals through a reform in social conditions?

Smith:– There is, in the end, no other way of prottecting them. The nation will do dirty and cruel work for no one. Surely, it is vain to expect men to treat the brutes humanely until they have ceased to deal with each other brutally.

Prevention of Cruelty Man:– What are you going to do with the vivisectionists?

Smith:– Vivisect them, I hope.

XXXI

Talks on Nationalism—To an Evolutionist

Mr. Smith, who has recently joined the nationalists, has a talk with an evolutionist who is an enthusiast as to the survival of the fittest.

Evolutionist:– It is a sufficient objection to nationalism that it guarantees to everybody an equal livelihood, without regard to difference in performance, only requiring that everybody should do what he or she can. That idea is dead against the doctrine of evolution.

Smith:– How do you make that out?

Evolutionist:– The main idea of evolution is the survival of the fittest as the result of the struggle for existence. Your plan would take all the struggle out of existence.

Smith:– I don't see that at all.

Evolutionist:– Why, if a fixed income for livelihood is guaranteed everyone who behaves decently, and he cannot get more in any event, what is there left for him to struggle for?

Smith:– As much as he had before. Did you ever observe that a man's contentedness had anything to do with the amount of his possessions or achievements?

178

TO AN EVOLUTIONIST

Did you ever hear of Alexander, who, having obtained the whole world, wept because he could not conquer another? There is no end to the desires and aspirations of the human heart. As fast as one is realized, another takes its place, an so on to infinity. Unless human nature suffers some unprecedented modification under nationalism, the energies now expended in competing for bread and butter will simply be expended, without diminution in intensity, in competing for other things.

Evolutionist:– But I understood there was to be no competition under nationalism.

Smith:– Who told you so?

Evolutionist:– Why, I understood that the abolition of competition was the main object of your plan.

Smith:– We propose to abolish what is technically called the competitive system of industry, but we do not propose to abolish competition. We could not, without abolishing human nature. So long as there are two persons in the world, whatever one of them does the other will try to do better, and that, too, even if vanity and envy should be no more known. Taking human nature just as it is, we believe that our plan for substituting the certain rewards of honor, authority and public approbation as incentives to diligence, for the wholly uncertain cash prizes now offered, will have the effect of stimulating every form of emulation beneficial to the public, while leaving other sorts of competition without a motive.

Evolutionist:– Ah, but you will never get men to compete for mere empty honors and promotion, as they now do for substantial gains.

Smith:– I think history is against you there. The

time was, not so very long ago, when it was thought necessary to reward soldiers with the plunder their valor had won, in order to encourage their zeal. They were permitted to sack cities and hold captives to ransom. War was then a gainful trade. All that is now changed. Only bandits and pirates fight for gain now. Whatever the army captures goes to the state, and the soldier is shot who is caught appropriating it. The only stimulus to the soldier's zeal is now the hope of distinction and promotion. According to your theory, this change ought to have ruined the efficiency of armies, but has it? Not only has the change not impaired the ardor of the soldier, but it has so ennobled his profession that instead of being a cut-throat and ruffian, as of old, he is today a respectable member of society. We are confident of a similar result from the plan of paying our workers in honor instead of in cash or in kind. We expect to see an intenser spirit of emulation on far higher grounds. We believe that the coming army of industry will be as much superior to the present mob of workers in efficiency as well as in morale, as the present German army is in both these respects to the hordes of Tilly and Wallenstein.

Evolutionist:-- You nationalists are a hopeful set, certainly.

Smith:-- Yes; we are the only people who have any right to be hopeful in the present condition of the world. But let us stick to evolution a little longer. You have been attacking nationalism from the ground of a believer in the theory that perfection comes out of struggle and the survival of the fittest.

TO AN EVOLUTIONIST

Evolutionist:– Well, that is true, is it not?

Smith:– Certainly; but there is an evolution of evil as well as of good. The wolf, the hyena, the rattlesnake and the shark are as striking results of the law of the survival of the fittest, as are the admirable types. The kind of fitness implied in the word "fit-test," as used in that phrase, is without any moral implication or reference to goodness or badness. It merely means fitness to the conditions of the struggle. If the conditions of the struggle are immoral and brutal, the most immoral and brutal types will survive. The issue then comes up on the question whether the conditions of the struggle under the present system of business tend to the survival of the nobler or the less noble types of human character. Upon the answer given to that question hangs the verdict whether the evolution favored by the present business system is toward social perfection or social damnation. What do you think?

Evolutionist:– I admit that the ethics of business are rather loose.

Smith:– You are bound to admit that there is no ethics in business, that ethics is bad business. Our business system is based on scientific selfishness, and is the negation of every generous, pitiful and public-spirited sentiment. Very many men in business, for the sake of their souls, fail to live up to this standard, but in so far they are poor business men. It is the debauching influence of the business system upon the public conscience, which more than anything else is holding back the moral progress of the people. What is the remedy? There is but one, and that is the one suggested by nationalism.

Replace the present business system with one the conditions of which shall encourage and give precedence to the nobler qualities of men instead of the meaner, and the same inexorable law of evolution, through the survival of those best fitted to their environment, which now tends to the degradation of society, will tend as strongly and irresistibly to its elevation.

XXXII

Talks on Nationalism—To a Dress Reformer

Mr. Smith, who has joined the nationalists, meets a dress reformer, and they discuss the relation of nationalism and fashion.

Smith:– I see that you are quoted as one of the leaders of this new movement for feminine dress reform.

Dress Reformer:– Yes; what do you think of it?

Smith:– Of its merits a good deal; as to its prospects of success I confess my hopes are greater than my expectations. Suppose you succeeded in bringing a better style of dress into favor, so that next season every woman from Maine to California followed it as closely as they do the present styles, what reason have you for supposing that it would prove more permanent than other styles have done?

Dress Reformer:– Because it would be more sensible.

Smith:– I'm afraid that would be a small assurance of permanence. There have been within the last score of years many styles of dress which, if not ideal, have been great improvements upon previous ones, but the sensible styles have not proved a whit more lasting than the others.

Dress Reformer:– That must be admitted.

TALKS ON NATIONALISM

Smith:– Seeing, then, that it is proved, if anything is, that the good sense of a fashion tends in no way to its permanence, why suppose that a style, merely because it is more sensible than any before it, should be lasting? So long as the usages of dress remain subject to the dictates of fashion, of which the essential principle is change for the sake of change, you dress reformers have rather a discouraging outlook.

Dress Reformer:– Dear me, that sounds distressingly as if it were true, and if it is, what hope is there for us poor women, for fashion will control us, I suppose, while we are human.

Smith:– I don't think that is at all necessary.

Dress Reformer:– I suppose you mean that your famous nationalism will put an end to its sway, but really that is asking us to believe too much.

Smith:– Well, let us inquire a little into that point. What is the secret strength of fashion? What is the reason, for some reason there must be, to account for the fact that all the women of the civilized world, two or three times a year, throw away their clothes and buy new ones, for no cause whatever connected with the use or beauty of the articles, but solely because the word is passed along that it is the fashion.

Dress Reformer:– I'm sure I don't know why they do it, and I don't think anybody else does.

Smith:– The problem by no means seems so hard as that. The senseless succession of fashions without the slightest pretense of any improvement, is accounted for by the fact that vast business interests, perhaps in their various ramifications constituting the largest single group

184

of manufactures and commerce, is devoted to the production and sale of articles of dress for men and women, chiefly women. The prosperity of these vast interests depends directly upon the amount of the goods they make and handle, which is consumed. The natural course of wear and tear would bring them in a certain amount of business, but they want more, and consequently seek to encourage the waste of clothing by every means possible.

Dress Reformer:– Your idea is, then, that the force at the bottom of fashion, which prompts the perpetual changes which it dictates, is the business interest of manufacturers and merchants?

Smith:– That is the basis of it. Add to this the equally direct and obvious interest of the great number of dressmakers, milliners and all others concerned in the purveying of articles of attire of any sort. Naturally those who desire clothing depend on the advice and counsel of this class, and it is as much their interest as that of the manufacturers themselves to stimulate their business by urging changes in style. The journals of fashion which are established to cater to the interest in fashion, in turn stimulate still further that interest by giving publicity to all news and gossip upon the subject. Their most liberal advertisers are, moreover, the merchants who deal in these same fashions.

Dress Reformer:– It would seem, then, that this whole business of fashion is a sort of conspiracy on the part of certain business interests against the welfare of the community.

Smith:– Oh, no; not a conspiracy. That would imply malice. It is only a combination of interests, the members of which are animated by no ill-will to the public, but merely by the natural desire of making a living. They are as worthy citizens as any other class of people in business; as good, in fact, as the business system will let them be. And now, do you see how nationalism would affect fashion?

Dress Reformer:– Why, naturally. The motive to stimulate the consumption of clothing as of all other things, will be lost when they are furnished to the people at cost.

Smith:– In another way, also. Ostentation is one of the strong motives of fashionable excesses. The existence of a class of wealthy women who have nothing else to do but to display their riches by a prodigal vanity of attire, has much to do with setting fashions. The economical equality which nationalism proposes, will of course put an end to such a class, and indeed will take away the motive of ostentation, for every one's income will be known to every one else.

Dress Reformer:– And under nationalism I suppose the fashions will never change.

Smith:– There will be no fashions then except those which commend themselves for their sense and beauty, and it holds to reason to suppose that they will only change when more sensible and attractive ones are invented.

Dress Reformer:– But who is going to do the inventing? I suppose we shall have to depend on the government and wear whatever it makes.

Smith:– If you did you could not be under a rule more

tyrannical than that you now obey, and it is certainly a libel on any imaginable government to suppose it would enforce such monstrosities as the magnates of fashion now do. But you would not be dependent on the government. No doubt there would then be as now the same choice between ready-made clothing and clothing made to order. It would be the interest of the government, if it were not to become unpopular, that the former grade should be as attractive as possible, while those who did not find it so would, as fastidious people now do, pay more for something made to order according to their own design or selection.

XXXIII

Looking Before and After

Editorial from The New Nation

WITH this number The New Nation enters upon its third year. Reform journalism is not pecuniarly profitable and ought not to be. If it were, its conductors would be quite too richly rewarded, at least nationalist papers would be; for certainly the dividends in growth and progress declared on our cause during the last two years have been such as to make it seem grasping to suggest the desirability of any other form of returns.

The progress of nationalism since 1890, and still more strikingly if we look back to the first organization of the nationalist propaganda in 1888, has exceeded the most sanguine anticipation of the most sanguine of our faith.

Look back four years and the United States was a practically virgin field for any form of the socialistic propaganda. Today, nationalism, the name given to the most radical form of socialism, nothing less than Jesus Christ's socialism, is a household word from one ocean to another. Four years ago, ridiculed as amiable enthusiasts, people actually fools enough to believe that God's kingdom of fraternal equality ever could come on earth, the nationalists today see their hope become the religion of hundreds of thousands, their practical program adopted as the creed of a national party which, having polled a million votes at its first election, in no spirit of idle boastfulness claims the presidency in 1896.

Public management of the railroads, the telegraphs, the telephones, the express service, the coal mines, the liquor traffic, the deposit and exchange banking system and of the issue of money, state insurance and the municipalization of all the public services of cities and towns, ideas scarcely heard of four years ago, many of them not two years ago, have become burning issues before national, state and municipal conventions and at the polls, and nowhere have the nationalists any other opposition to meet than that of mere inertia. The moral sentiment and the business sense are so absolutely and wholly on their side in every proposition they have made, that a hearing is all they have needed to ask for.

Ridicule was the only weapon that greed and ignorance could use against us from the start and that, long since dulled, we are turning against them with newly whetted edge. Our cause is instinctively recognized even by those who have not yet joined us, as that of all against the few, of the masses against the classes, the people against the plutocrats. We have everywhere put the other side on the defensive.

Can there be any question as to the future of such a party, which seeks the ideal of Christ by the most hardheaded sort of economic logic?

Parties of radical social reform in Europe and Great Britain antedated ours, and until recently it has appeared that America would be a laggard in the glorious race. The prospect has changed of late. America, aroused in time to recognize the falsity of its democratic pretensions, will yet be first to touch the goal of true liberty, equality and fraternity.

There are those who sigh for heroic days. There never was an epoch with such opportunities and demands for heroism and self-devotion as are offered by these passing years, when human destiny is turning as on a hinge.

There is no question of the speedy triumph of our cause; the only question, and it is a noble competition, is, who of us shall sacrifice most for it in the short time while it shall yet need self-sacrifice, before all men flock to its banner?

EDWARD BELLAMY, Editor.

January 7, 1893.

"But democracy has not yet made the world safe against irrational revolution. That supreme task, which is nothing less than the salvation of civilization, now faces democracy, insistent, imperative. There is no escaping it, unless everything we have built up is presently to fall in ruin about us; and the United States, as the greatest of democracies, must undertake it."
  —Woodrow Wilson in The Atlantic Monthly, (August, 1923).

Date Due

NOT RTD JUN 28 2006			

IF YOUR BOOK IS RECALLED YOUR DUE
DATE WILL BE SHORTENED. YOU WILL BE
NOTIFIED BY MAIL.